Groping
for
Support

When Death Strikes Far Away

Rev. Dr. Joseph M. Kimatu

WESTBOW
PRESS®
A DIVISION OF THOMAS NELSON
& ZONDERVAN

WestBow Press books may be ordered through booksellers or by contacting:

WestBow Press
A Division of Thomas Nelson & Zondervan
1663 Liberty Drive
Bloomington, IN 47403
www.westbowpress.com
844-714-3454

ISBN: 978-1-6642-7917-9 (sc)
ISBN: 978-1-6642-7916-2 (e)

Print information available on the last page.

WestBow Press rev. date: 10/12/2022

Contents

Dedication

I dedicate this book to the thousands of God's children, young and old who suffer and grieve in isolation and silence, because they do not have a chance to witness the burial of their loved ones. The distance and immigration have been a real impediment. Thanks to those who reach out for their Groping Hands and offer support.

My dear Mama
I will live to remember your love,
I will never forget how you brought me up.
You cared for me and supplied my needs,
you represented God to me.
Forgive me for not being there, to say
my final goodbye to you.
Forgive me for not being there,
when they lowered you into your final resting home.
If I had wings, I could fly,
but I am sure you will understand me mama.
Someday I'll see you,
someday soon I'll join you,
This time we will never separate again,
I love you, Mama.

Acknowledgments

This book would not have been a success without the support of many people and institutions through the course of the past several years. A few paragraphs are not enough for me to express my gratitude to all those involved, but I will do the best I can to thank all of them. If perchance I miss out on anyone, it is not by intention.

First and foremost, I would like to thank my family. To my wife, Jane, I say a big thank you. Her encouragement, her input and painstaking patience to sit with me for long hours far into the night deserve unreserved commendation. No one else could have done this for me.

I would also like to thank her for the extra hard work she did to keep our children healthy and strong especially towards the final stages of writing this book. Not one of our children complained. You made them understand the process. On top of it all, you made them desire to see the work completed. Thank you, Dominic, Marylily and Silvia my wonderful children, your support, love and understanding kept me going even when fatigue threatened to take the better of me.

Much gratitude goes to my mentor and advisor, the Rev. Dr. John Webster and his loving wife, Penny. Thank you, my reviewers for your guidance, direction and support; you carefully read and wrote detailed comments on my drafts.

This substantially contributed to the fine-tuning of this project.

You also shaped the direction that opened a completely new dimension of giving care to people living in two different worlds. For all your contributions, I am grateful beyond what words can express. I highly appreciate your encouragement and for sure I am indebted.

Special thanks go to Rev. Dr. Melton Loyd of Erskine Theological Seminary, Due West, South Carolina, for helping and supervising me through the writing of my Dissertation, Mourning without the Body: Pastoral Care and Support to those Mourning in Isolation. This book is a product of the Dissertation approved towards my achieving a doctoral degree. Thank you for your good work. I am very proud of you.

I would also like to thank the congregations at Tumaini Community Church, Imani Presbyterian Church, Ushindi Presbyterian and my former congregation, First Presbyterian Church in Atlanta, and the Presbyterian Church USA in general, for supporting me materially, spiritually, and morally throughout my course of study and hence facilitating the compilation of this book.

Special thanks go to the former executive presbyter of my immediate former presbytery, the Presbytery of Southern New England, The Reverend Dana Lindsley. You stood with me during the final laps of compiling this work. I cannot stop before thanking The Rev. Dr. George Worth and Rev. Connie Lee of First Presbyterian Church in Atlanta who were very helpful in many ways during my entire graduate studies.

To both of you and several others at FPC, receive my special thanks. I am also very thankful to Dr. Melva Costen, my former advisor at the Interdenominational Theological Center in Atlanta, and Dr. Carolyn McCrary for inspiring, urging me on and encouraging me to take on this task.

The three friends and close confidants who assisted me in picking a group of eight members who worked with me in the process are highly appreciated and I thank them for their discernment. On the same note, I would like to thank the group of eight who willingly and voluntarily worked with me and with each other and participated fully in making this project possible. Without their zeal, effort and contribution, this book would not have seen the light of the day.

To all others who have not been mentioned, I am deeply indebted for your prayers and encouragement, surely you wished me well. Receive special thanks from the bottom of my heart for the valuable part you played in making this venture a success.

Preface

This book is a result of a project that the pastor (the author himself) mutually carried out with a group of some church members who had suffered losses of loved ones and they were not able to be there when they died and what followed after that.

The project proper involved eight members of a church and their pastor who facilitated the process. The group met on six occasions and went through a series of activities. The group members and the pastor had one thing in common. Each had lost a member or members of their family and were not able to be present to see the body/bodies or participate in the funeral and burial processes.

The group met and went through sharing and discussion sessions. The group performed some rituals and observed moments of high emotional outbursts. At last, a sample list of some ways to assist those in similar circumstances was compiled and a desire to form support groups after undergoing training was expressed.

A major part of the book comprises a lengthy explanation of the understanding of death, funeral, and burial process within the Kikuyu group of peoples. Included also is a chapter on the main resources used. Another chapter contains a discussion on the best way to approach the project. A chapter on the theological rationale for the project is included and finally an evaluation section concludes this work.

My hope is that this book will help in the process and bring better results to pastors and other religious leaders. It will be a useful tool to help those of their members who mourn and grieve without the body and in isolation from the rest of their close family members. The reason being because, they are either undocumented immigrants or immigrants who have lost their statuses.

They have lost the capacity to travel back to their country, but one thing is for sure, they have not lost the capacity to grieve and mourn. They are human just like anyone else. When calamity comes to their shores, especially when their loved ones die abroad, they deserve support. Sometimes it is not forth coming or is not enough, so they are left groping for it, hence the title of this book, "Groping for Support." The title of this book alludes to that very fact.

The Unfortunate Many

A group of eight people was involved in carrying out the project. The group met for five sessions after the initial brainstorming and planning meeting. Those involved shared their responses and gave feedback to others' responses on an already agreed to questionnaire. They also participated in several rituals.

At the end of the process, they did an evaluation of its importance and value. The group was so inspired that a desire to further get equipped and to form some new grief support groups was expressed. To be of immediate help to others, the group came up with a "to do list" that can be used to help people in grief situations.

The author also contacted and interviewed some pastors who are in active ministry in their congregations. Out of the several who were interviewed, only one had a system in place to deal with crisis of loss for those who were unable to travel to see their loved ones buried.

The exceptional pastor did not have a structured method of dealing with the problem, but at least he was willing to fill out and return the questionnaire sent out to all to fill. All the other pastors shied away from writing anything on paper and getting back to the author.

I talked with them, some face to face and others on other media. While talking with them, I detected I could have assumed too much. The majority were reluctant because they were afraid of their lack of adequacy in handling situations where their members cry out, "I need some support" would be apparent.

Two of the pastors were honest enough to say, "They felt it safe leaving it to the family and friends to handle it although they admitted not promoting the same. A few said they had other more pressing problems and issues on their ministerial plate.

Two of the pastors lead multi-racial congregations. They reasoned that each of the racial/community group was left to do it in its own way. Since each did something unique when a death happens, they reasoned that letting the group free to do what they knew best would be a good way of dealing with its particular loss.

This felt to me like shirking responsibility if not spreading it around in an uncontrolled manner. I am of the assumption that we should not leave things to chance. As pastors we should be more involved. Death is a serious matter. After all, are we not risk takers?

To the above I would say, grief is grief regardless of who is suffering. Grief knows no race and does not discriminate between communities. At least there must be a way the church can be helpful. A pastor who cares should not leave such matters as pertains to the loss of a loved one, a child, a spouse, a parent, or a friend to chance.

If a school counsels its students after a shooting or an accident; if companies hire professionals, counselors, and chaplains to provide support during the loss of one or more of its employees; if hospitals engage chaplains to support and comfort families, patients, friends, staffs and colleagues in crisis situations, what institution is better placed to go an extra mile to support its members than the church itself?

In such matters, the church should be the leader and not the follower, the head and not the tail. Members come to the church because they expect their spiritual needs will be met by the church community led by its leaders. Their trust, their hope, their strength is expected to come from the faith community.

If the leaders of such communities have nothing in place, it is possible they will have many followers who will be sick from internalized and unaddressed grief. Nowhere else is grief greater than in someone who loses a close relative, and they are not able to travel and participate in bidding them goodbye or to mourn with the others and to "close" together with their loved ones.

This is the plight of many immigrants who reside in the United States. Many of them are not able to travel back to their countries of origin when one or more of their close relatives pass on. They fear to leave the country because if they did, that's it, they will not be able to reenter the country that they love.

Many have no papers or whatever papers they had have expired. Their fate is therefore sealed; stay put, grieve, and mourn your loss. These people cry for help. They call out loud for support. Is it asking too much for churches and other religious institutions to come out with at least an instrument or at least something to assist these sufferers?

As I write, I remember this woman who called me. She has never met me but knew of me from a friend who knows me as one who stands with those who suffer. After crying over the phone for a long while and later apologizing for doing it with a stranger, to which I replied she deserved it and needed not to feel sorry, she shared with me some very sad news. Her first, and only son, was very sick and was hospitalized that morning after suffering a massive heart failure. His life was hanging by a thread.

She feared the worst. Her daughter in law had been told by the doctor, it was next to impossible that he was going to survive. My caller is in the United States. Her family is all in her country of origin. The last time she saw any of them was 15 years ago. Although her being in the United States has been beneficial to her raising and educating her family of five, she felt regretful she left them.

She felt guilt at not being there for her son and of cause; she cannot be because her immigration papers are not in order. She has already long overstayed her visitor's visa. If she were to leave, she is unlikely ever to return to this country that she loves. One of her children is in a university abroad and she would like to see her through.

Her worst fear is that her son would die, and she would not be there to bid him farewell before he passed. She also fears that she herself would die with grief and guilt. This woman was "groping for support." Doesn't her church where she has invested and entrusted her life have something in place for her? There are a lot of people like her, groping for support every day even as I write. This book offers some suggestions on how churches can help satisfy this need.

Jane is the middle child in her family and the favorite child of his late dad. She was so close to her dad that even at age eleven, her dad used to bathe her. Her dad unfortunately did not live long. When she was 19, he passed away, leaving her devastated and as she says, "half her heart died". The other half only stayed alive because of her mother. When all her siblings got married and some left home to work in the city, she was left behind to take care of her mother. Both developed some very close relationship. She describes her mother as, "a sister, a friend and a mother" Jane took great care of her mom and especially when she needed support most. One fateful wintry day in September 1997, she slipped, fell down and broke her hip. Jane took care of her until Jane turned fifty. After her successful career in the public service in Kenya, Jane was awarded, together with a few of her colleagues, a special treat by her ministry.

She came to the United States on a visitor's visa on a fully paid tour. She fell in love with the country and visited more than ten states at the invitation of her friends and relatives. She didn't notice time was fast flying and by the time she became conscious of her circumstances, she realized she had overstayed her visa.

Unlike many others who are not as fortunate, she was able to tap into and get a slice of the American dream. After a few years, she had settled down and rented a single family house. Jane was all the time thinking about her mother back home. She missed her a lot and so started to figure out how to bring her over to the United States.

She tried all ways and with the help of her siblings, she was able to obtain the necessary papers to help her travel to the U. S. She had the house and so the only thing she had to do was to buy the necessary stuff for her mother's bedroom. She also filled her closet with clothes and all she needed to use during her stay. She went to the extent of constructing a wheel-chair ramp to ferry her mom in and out of the house. She remodeled her bathroom to make it suitable for her use. She had all in place and just waited pleasurably and with great anticipation for her arrival after she had paid for her ticket.

A day before her travel, calamity struck and true to the saying, it did not come singly. Her mother fell seriously sick and was admitted into a hospital. At exactly the scheduled time of her flight the next day, she succumbed to her illness and died. Jane was on the phone almost all the time with her family in Kenya monitoring her progress and when the news of her death reached her, she felt her whole world crumble under her feet. As she puts it, the other half of her heart died. Her only parent was no more.

Seven years later, Jane is still mourning the loss of her mother. She is still in shock and denial. The room she had done for her is still there, furniture undisturbed, closet untouched, the ramp intact and the bathroom ready for her use.

Jane is still waiting for her mother to come to her. Every passing day increases her anxiety as she hopes what she heard was not true. She lives like someone in a dream, this time an unending dream. The thoughts of her mother dying are foreign. Her mother still exists somewhere on this earth, in her home in Kenya.

Jane was unable to travel back to Kenya to see the dead body of her beloved mother. She was neither able to be present nor to participate in the funeral rites and rituals that come before and after the burial. Jane missed all those key observances and still believes her mother is alive.

Jane could not travel to Kenya because she knew her reentry would not be allowed. The sad fact is that to this day, Jane is still mourning her mother. This is a true story, but the name is fictitious in order to preserve Jane's privacy.

Kevin, not his real name came to the United States when he was barely twenty. He had just graduated from High School. Both her parents, siblings and friends escorted him to the airport to see him off. They kissed him goodbye, and he boarded his flight. That was twenty years ago and the last time he was ever to see his parents alive.

Kevin came to the United States to study. The first three years were great. This was not to last. In the middle of the fourth year, a few months before his graduation from college, his father fell sick, his condition deteriorated, and he finally died. Kevin lost his father's financial support and he fell out of school.

Kevin received some financial support from the members of his small church and friends. All what was raised was sent home to his mother, to assist her in the funeral of his dad. After a week of mourning, no one came back to him to check out how he was doing. Life went on as if nothing had happened. He was left struggling on his own.

Kevin had been out of school for long and so his student visa expired, and he lost his immigrant status. For two years he struggled to keep afloat. He survived for a few months being supported by friends here and there. But unfortunately, they could not meet all his needs. For two years he did odd jobs in various places in an effort to make ends meet. He lost many of his friends who saw him as a burden to them and some even shunned him.

His mother was devastated by the loss of her husband. Her grief went from stress to depression, and she developed very serious episodes of high blood pressure. Kevin had to sustain his mother from the little earnings he received from the sporadic low paying jobs he did. Three and a half years after the demise of her husband, Kevin's mother was found still and cold in her bed. She died of a massive heart attack. Poor Kevin was now an orphan.

This was the worst blow Kevin had ever had. He was still out of status and could not travel back to Kenya to bury his mother. His grief this time round escalated almost beyond what he could bear. Kevin almost gave up living altogether. Life almost lost value and he felt like taking away his life. He regretted that moment that he left home.

Kevin's Church and community came together to help him out, but they were there for him for a short time. After about a week, the church and friends once again faded out, but his grief did not. It lingered on and it seemed there was no end to it. Since that time, Kevin has been crying for support, o yea, groping for support. He described his condition to me as a living nightmare.

The writing of this book was inspired by the suffering, pain and grief of people like Jane and Kevin. Jane and Kevin are representatives of a huge number of immigrants in this country, who for various reasons are not able to rejoin their families at such critical moments like Jane's and Kevin's.

These people suffer in silence because the reality of what transpired in their absence is hard to actualize. The purpose of writing this book is to seek ways in which people like Jane and Kevin can find support and help on their journey of "mourning without the body" so as to initiate healing and recovery on their part.

It is also purposed that when they have recovered, they can be of use to others who may be in or will be facing similar experiences in the future. That is what is at the heart of this book. The book is also intended to be a useful tool to pastors and caregivers whose members/ clients face similar predicaments.

2

Honoring the Dead

Sometimes, the honor given to the dead body of a person is greater than that the person was given when s/he was alive. It may be argued that we give the dead a special treatment because it is their last. Perhaps it can also be suggested that we want to repay the honor that we did not accord them when they were with us. But all said and done, there is something that happens when a relative passes on, that calls for some inquisitiveness.

The key area for investigation is why we give this honor and what happens to some of us when and if we do not. This book attempts to find some answers to these questions. A group of eight persons together with their pastor are involved in the project proper. All of them originally hail from the same country, region, tribe, and ethnic group. They also lived in the same geographical area, belonged to the same church, and had suffered a loss of one or more of their relatives back in Kenya. Neither of them was able to travel to Kenya to be present during the funeral process. The project focuses on their mourning without the body and experiments on how to help them heal and recover from their grief.

The author of this book was born and raised in the central region of Kenya and speaks from experience during his life in his community as well as his ministry as a pastor in the same region. The writer's argument is also informed from books written about African traditions and philosophy especially by Dr. John S. Mbiti and the late Mr. Jomo Kenyatta, who also became Kenya's first president, amongst other writers.

Mbiti is an authority on African religions and philosophy. Kenyatta is a well-known writer on Kikuyu traditions and customs. Both authors have been relied upon heavily.

Until recently, it was anathema, and/or shame altogether, to even imagine, let alone to attempt burying the remains of a dead person in a public cemetery. This was tantamount to being disrespectful of the dead. It was taken as throwing away or trashing an unwanted person just as you would a carcass.

Public cemeteries were for the foreigners who had no local family connections, or for unknown casualties of war. Most of them (cemeteries) mushroomed in cities after the two World Wars of 1914-18 and 1939-45. African soldiers who died fighting alongside their colonial masters had their remains or parts of them brought home and buried in these war-veterans' cemeteries.

Strangers, who had no known local links, in very rare cases, were also buried in these cemeteries. Others were the unclaimed or unwanted by any family or clan, plus the homeless or street people who had scanty community attachments.

There was a common belief that if a clan or family failed to send their dead ones away in a respectful, honorable and decent way, their spirits will be "scorned and displeased" and would therefore, come back seeking vengeance and to punish or haunt those that failed to honor them.

It was also seen as dishonorable for a clan or family not to accord as much respect and treatment to the remains of their dead ones. If such a thing happened, such a unit of people would become the scorn of the community and not many people would like to associate with them. Their girls and men would find it very difficult to find a suitor or someone to ask for their hand in marriage from the larger community.

No one would dream of becoming a pariah or scorn of the community. There were a time people were afraid of touching a dead body lest they become unclean. People who became very sick and seemed like they would never recover or were near death were taken outside the home and into the forest or bushes and left out there to die.

A fire would be lit for them to keep warm and some food and water so that they would not die from cold, hunger or thirst. It they recovered; they were welcomed back into the community. If they died, they became food for hyenas and other scavengers. But those are days far gone.

Today, if such a thing happened it would make news all over the world. Dead bodies are respected and disposed of in dignity. The fear of getting near or touching dead bodies has long been rooted out.

The World of the Dead

In the African belief, the spirit world (world of the dead) is not divorced or separated from the world of the living. John Mbiti in his book, *African Religions and Philosophy*, describes the scenario of the world (our present sphere) as not only a world of the living, but also a world where the departed were constantly or perpetually in communion with the living. He says,

Death is conceived of as a departure and not complete annihilation of a person. He moves on to join the company of the departed, and the only major change is decay of the physical body, but the spirit moves on to another state of existence".[1]

Mbiti goes on to show how significant the communion between the dead and the living is. When the communion is healthy, all is well. If the communion becomes sore or conflictive, calamities (sickness, death, losses of flock, crop or other property) would befall the living.

To appease the spirits, they were treated well. Libations were done to cement relations. The spirits of key departed ones were invoked when the family sought for blessings or protection against evil forces. This belief in the communion of the departed souls and the living, parallels the Christian belief in the "communion of saints" (cf. the Apostles Creed). Paul's argument (1 Thess. 4: 13-18) at the end of time sometimes referred to as the "Parousia" (Parousia is a Greek name interpreted as the return of Christ and the rising of the dead to commune with the living as they are caught up in the air) is no different. It is also not unlike the "resurrection" of Christ. His risen body/ form communed with the early Christians (disciples).

They ate together, talked together, and broke the bread together.

He would then disappear, even with doors closed, through the wall, like a spirit. It is amazing that the gospel writers did not question this happening. They record that he appeared to them as a ghost. Such stories are not uncommon

---

[1] John S. Mbiti, *African Religions and Philosophy* (London: Heinemann Educational Books, 1979), 157.

Rev. Dr. Joseph M. Kimatu

in many African societies. Feeding the spirits of the dead and offering sacrifices to them is a common practice within many communities.

Jesus' promise of sending the Spirit, the Spirit of the Father and himself, sounds familiar and resonates with the African belief of "the spirit world" invading and permeating the world of the living. Hence, the concept / meaning of Immanuel is akin to the African idea of communion with the "living-dead".

There are many stories of individuals and families who claim to have been visited by spirits of their dead ones. They even claim the spirits requested for certain favors and those visited also made their requests. Such families would prepare special meals and share them with the spirits of the dead. After such interactions the family and the spirit (living dead) would rest in peace.

The family would be assured of blessings and prosperity and protection and for some time, no interference. These concepts can be found in the Old Testament and the New Testament as well. Two Old Testament figures appear in the story of the Transfiguration in the New Testament. This is a good example of "The dead visiting the living." Moses and Elijah (long dead but still in peoples' memory are very significant figures in Jewish religious history) both appeared and stood with the living Jesus on the high mountain (Mark 9: 1-13).

The three disciples who were with Jesus, Peter, James and John, recognized the characters appearing with Jesus though they had never seen them before. Both Moses and Elijah lived centuries of years before the time of Jesus on earth. The author of Mark also tells the story so naturally as if it was not something unheard of before then.

The Jewish community had been long waiting for the return of Elijah and even kept a special place for him during the Passover maybe with the notion that his spirit was present with them. When Jesus died, as the story goes, he descended into hell and then came back to the world of the living. It is like he connected the living and the dead and through him, both worlds became one. He is both God of the living and the dead.

The Kikuyu people have very similar beliefs. They also name some children after those who have passed and somehow believe that in those so named, the one who passed on has been resurrected. Some common Kikuyu names have this kind of interpretation: *Kariuki* means one who has resurrected, *Muchoki* means one who has come back, *Wairiuko* means one associated with the one who has risen, *Njoki* means one who has returned, *Muriuki* means the risen one, and so on.

Someone said, if one wanted to convert somebody to Christianity using the least persuasion, let him/her go to Africa. The phenomena of Christianity have many parallels with the African beliefs about this-life and its relationship with the afterlife. The fact that Christianity has been and is still growing rapidly in the African continent, especially south of the Sahara, cannot be better explained.

The president of the All-Africa Conference of Churches (AACC), The Reverend Nyansako-ni-Nku, in his interview with the Highlights, a magazine of the *Presbyterian Church (U.S.A), Worldwide Ministries Division*, made this comment about the religiosity of the African people as his answer to the reason why the church in Africa is fast growing:

> Some people have described Africans as incurably religious. Religion is so embedded in Africans' culture and way of life that when missionaries came they didn't introduce the worship of God. They were not saying

something that was very, very new to Africans. What was new was the kind of worship and the definition of God". [2]

Mbiti describes, and rightly so, Africans being "notoriously religious". Every aspect of the African life has religious meaning. He uses this imagery to explain his point: "From eating to marriage, from rites of passage to the passing of a person, rituals accompany all the events of the African life".

The rites and the corresponding rituals were done according to the understanding of the event for which they were designed. It is therefore necessary to understand the African general concept of death. Mbiti has this to say about death:

> From funeral rites and methods of disposing with the dead body, we can catch glimpses of African concepts of death. Burial is the most common method of dealing with the corpse and different customs are followed. Some societies bury the dead inside the house where the person was living before s/he died; others bury it in the compound where the homestead is situated; others bury the dead behind the compound; and some do so at the place where the person was born. In some areas there is the custom to bury food, weapons, stools, tobacco, clothing, and formerly one's wife or wives, so that these may accompany the departed to the next world. [3]

---

[2] Mbiti, 1.
[3] Mbiti, 158.

To paraphrase Mbiti: Sometimes the body would be preserved for several months before burial. Some part of the body, a jawbone, skull, or other part could be kept back by the family as a protective charm, or as a living reminder that the departed person is still present with the family.

The measure of honor and respect given to the departed sometimes was dependent on the deceased's position in society and the family, his/her age and at times gender.

Mbiti goes on to explain the view Africans had on death:

> Again it is clear that people view death paradoxically: it is a separation but not annihilation. The dead person is suddenly cut off from the human society and yet the corporate group clings to him. This is shown through the elaborate funeral rites, as well as other methods of keeping in contact with the departed. At the moment of physical death the person becomes the living-dead: he's neither alive physically, nor dead relative to the corporate group. His own Sasa period is over, he enters fully into the Zamani period, but as far as the living who knew him are concerned, he is kept "back" in the Sasa period, from which he can disappear only gradually. Those who have nobody to keep them in the Sasa period in reality "die" immediately, which is a great tragedy that must be avoided at all costs. [4]

If one were to read Mbiti well, it seems like the passage into the other world can be hastened or halted by the activities

---

[4] Ibid., 159.

of the living as well as how they held the departed in their hearts and memory.

Burial is a serious rite and the better it is done, the better is the journey the departed is engaged in. It is as though the acceptance of the departed into the "next world" depended on how well the living handled the transition. Any good or ill will on the part of the living had consequences on the latter life of the departed.

Where One Is Buried Matters

These beliefs and understandings are not lost on the present generations. They are further strengthened by the presence of graves in almost all homesteads in the country (Kenya). It is held to be of paramount importance that every adult male individual should at least possess a piece of land where he will be buried when he dies.

This is seen as a way of ensuring that the spirit remains connected with the family. The best way to be buried, however, is in one's indigenous clan/family graveyard. This is the most ideal place to be interred unless one expresses a wish to be buried elsewhere, which is very rare.

The will is binding as long as the clan/family has no dispute over or a problem with it. In Kenya, some of the most famous "court cases" are of disputes over the burial place of individuals whose spouse's choice of the location of burial goes against the grain of beliefs and practices of the clan/family.

In the mind of most Kenyans are the unforgettable and notable S.M. Otieno and P.C. Mburu sagas (the former a judge of the high court and the latter, a former provincial commissioner), amongst many others. These two cases were held in the early 80's. They were so prolonged and hotly contested and still remain fresh in the minds of many who lived then to this day. It is as if they happened yesterday. It is in the constitution of the land that in civil matters, if the law conflicts with the traditional customs, the latter takes precedence over the former.

It is not uncommon for remains to go for many months before they are buried due to the prolonged court cases and the appeals that follow before the verdicts are determined. Most of these cases are between the dead person's spouse and the clan the dead spouse belonged.

It is critical where one is buried since connection with the departed does not cease with the burial. A recent story in a Kenyan newspaper, reported about a woman who was buried almost a year after her death. The woman was allegedly murdered by her bodyguard. This woman was the wife of a former Mũngĩkĩ leader. (Mũngĩkĩ since proscribed is a Kikuyu underground cultural movement in Kenya that is allegedly associated with causing mayhem, murder, and other criminal activities in the country.

This man was in jail when his wife was murdered. Her body was preserved in a mortuary until he was released, and it was only after his release that the body was given to him for burial. Her funeral was one of the most well attended funerals in the country. If she was buried when her spouse was in jail, this would have been held as tantamount to dishonor and disrespect. Her position in society would have been downgraded from being a wife to being a concubine if not less.

It is also common practice to transport bodies of people who die abroad back to Kenya in order for them to be buried in their proper burial places. Kenyans contribute a lot of money to ensure this happens and it is only in very exceptional cases that the practice is not put in force.

According to the stories of fundraisings for funerals

among the Kenyan community living in the United States, a popular news media website (Ajabu Africa), for Africans living in this country, once reported over $200,000.00 was raised in the year (2009) alone to meet funeral expenses for Kenyans who passed on in the US and whose bodies were to be transported to Kenya for burial. Other media outlets, Samrack, Mwakilishi, Diaspora Media, Diaspora Messenger, Jamhuri Magazine, radio, TV, and WhatsApp groups have become avenues for death announcements, and fundraisings to ship the bodies back home. The amounts of money spent has since raised if not quadrupled.

Over the years, the community is still raising more to do the same, repatriate bodies back to Kenya. Even those who live in small and isolated cities are not left out. Our social media houses connect us and when they are bereaved, they are helped out by the rest of the folk living in bigger cities.

Perhaps a casual observer or a small minority in the community would ask, "Why not look for alternative ways of getting rid of the bodies of our dead rather than this expensive practice of transferring them back to Kenya?

Why not simply cremate them or bury them in local cemeteries?"

Cremation is a new concept to many in the Kenyan communities. We used to hear it associated with Indians. Indians have been living in Kenya for a long time dating back to the late 1890s. India and Kenya were colonies of Britain. When the British were constructing the Kenya-Uganda railway line (variously referred to by its builders as the "lunatic express" and the locals as the iron-snake) from Mombasa to Kampala, they brought (most likely by force) 32,000 Indian laborers all the way from India to help construct the railway.

We used to read in our history classes that they were called coolies (unskilled laborer or porter). Many of these Indians did not return to India after the railway was completed. They settled in Kenya and started retail shops; they became Duka-Wallas, artisans, traders, clerks, and government workers. Today, in Kenya, there are many citizens of Indian descent a number that is estimated to be over 100,000.

The Indians in Kenya have long been cremating their dead. Rumor had it that after cremation, they would take the ashes, spread them out in nearby big rivers in the hope that the river waters would finally end up in the Indian Ocean that forms the Kenya coastline. The ashes would end up in the Indian Ocean waters and the Monsoon winds would help carry them back to India and to their final resting place.

Cremation is a rare if not a strange practice. It is still very hard to sell or convince the idea to many Kenyans and of course most other African communities. It is easier to bring the Kenyan community together and for them to raise tens of thousands of US dollars to send corpses back to Kenya than to convince them to raise a few thousands to cremate the body in the US or in whatever other country they have migrated to. From the look of things, it will be a long time before the practice is embraced. It is a hard sell and will remain so for the next few decades. Though some Kenyans live in the Diaspora, they remain "the property" of their relations back in Kenya and this is more pronounced when they die.

There have been cases of dead children, who were born in the US and have never been to Kenya, being transported in coffins to be buried there. There have also been cases where parents of natural born children in the US, children who will never go back to Kenya, being transported to Kenya when they die. Their children will never have a chance to go and lay flowers on their graves any time. The idea or belief that even dead bodies, let alone living ones belong to their communities will take a long time to die. If resurrection will be bodily, some will not recognize where they are, ha!

Funerals and burials are community responsibilities and activities. That means that whenever one dies, it is not just the family that is involved. The clan, community, friends, colleagues, the church, associates, and friends of the deceased as well as the bereaved close family members are actively involved. Mourners from miles around come for the burial ceremony not by invitation, but on their own volition.

They come to both witness and grace the occasion as well as to support the family by their presence and to honor and celebrate the life of the departed. They also contribute to defray the funeral costs as well as to give material and financial support to the family that has been left behind. It matters little one's status in life. The numbers of mourners may vary, but it rests on the community to bury their dead. In Kenya there is nothing like a "private funeral service". If anyone ever conducted one, it would be taken as an irresponsible act, a disgrace to the community, and it would earn the wrath of the whole community.

It would be a headliner in the news and such a person will be seen as "abnormal", weird and absurd and many folks would come to fear and detest him/her. Perhaps it will create better understanding if I were to explain the process that takes place after one dies until the time s/ he is paid the last respects at the gravesite. The process takes between five and fourteen days, depending on the availability of the religious figure who officiates at the burial and how soon close relatives who live afar can travel to be present on the day of the funeral.

If for instance, some relatives of the dead person live in the United States, the funeral can be delayed by a week to await their arrival. Unless it is impossible due to unforeseen circumstances or circumstances beyond one's control, the presence of the whole family is the ideal thing. There are rituals that are critical in the funeral and burial process that every member of the family (by family, the African understanding is the western idea of extended family) be present. The importance of one's presence is explained in the next chapter in detail.

In conclusion, let me reiterate that the world of the living and the dead has no clear demarcation or distinction. It is sort of merged into one. It is also important that the dead is buried with all the proper rituals in place. The family farm is the most ideal resting place. It is the community's responsibility to ensure that the deceased's family is supported and comforted and the deceased's body is buried with the honor it deserves. In the next chapter, we shall investigate what takes place when someone dies and the process ensuing from the event.

3

What Follows Death

Given the luxury of choosing the circumstances around which one would wish to die, a lot of Kikuyu people would choose to pass on when all their family members are around them. This is because when one passes on, the death ushers in a series of events that require the family to be together for a while. There is also great comfort when the family surrounds a dying relative on his/her death bed, not just to the one passing, but also to the family.

This accords both parties a time to say goodbye to each other and leaves behind good memories for the family to remember the one passing on. It feels like escorting him/her on his journey and it also gives the notion s/he is still with us. Unfortunately, this is not always the case. Only a few fortunate families experience or witness this golden opportunity. To the dismay of many, most folk die when their families are scattered all over the country, sometimes even abroad.

The departure of a loved one sets a series of things into motion. The deceased's relative(s) who first get the sad news communicate to the family members who in turn communicate to others. Within a short time (a day or two), the majority of the family members would have gotten the information. As soon as it is practically possible, the closest of relatives would meet at the deceased's home. If the deceased lived in a city, home would be his parent's residence.

Africans differentiate between a home and a house. The house is one's residence away from his ancestral area and the home is the place where his ancestors lived. At the home of the deceased, the family members would meet to comfort, support, encourage and condole with each other.

The parents, spouse, siblings, children, and grandparents would be the primary recipients of most of the care and attention. The family would then consult with each other and determine what needed to be done; in other words, the way forward.

Without invitation, friends, distant relatives, and the immediate community, would come on their own volition, to the home of the deceased. A funeral committee would be formed. The committee comprising a chairman, a secretary, a treasurer amongst others would be charged with the planning of the funeral and burial of the deceased. The committee would work closely with the family and the clan.

The committee will come up with a budget. The cost of the funeral, entertainment, transportation, hospital bills and other financial obligations that the deceased left behind, would be put into consideration. This funeral committee would also in consultation with the family suggest the appropriate date for the funeral. Their suggestion would be forwarded to the pastor or other religious leaders responsible for the burial.

Once an agreement has been reached, announcements are then made by word of mouth and media both print and electronic, and mostly by radio. The church, as the place where most community activities are centered, also becomes very much involved in the process. The church organizes for prayers every evening until the day of the burial.

Ecumenical Spirit

There is no better manifestation of ecumenism than during such daily prayer sessions. All denominations are involved, and they participate in the various components of the worship service. Space is provided for those who want to sing, give a testimony, greet the worshipers, and convey a condolence message, and all other activities that are of value to the mourners.

Pastors and civic leaders, who turn up to mourn with the family are also given a chance to speak. One might by now be wondering how long the prayers last. In most cases, it is no less than three hours if not more. Beyond caring for the family spiritually, this "new community" formed around the demise of the dead person also does much more other than just pray.

The mourners donate money to meet funeral and other expenses. The community also provides food for everyone who comes to the deceased's home. Those who own vehicles or other necessary things needed for the funeral offer them for use most of the time without asking for any compensation.

The family is helped in all ways possible. The funeral becomes a community task other than a family burden. The family is relieved from all duties and in so doing is given a chance to mourn their loss. The family is also accorded time to comfort each other and to be in fellowship. This time becomes a time when close family relationships are rekindled.

The family centers on their grief and has not much to do other than being consulted on issues that the funeral committee deems necessary. It is not uncommon for some funeral rites to be observed during this period. It mostly depends on the family and the clan that the deceased comes from. The rites would also depend on the last wishes of the deceased. Most of these rituals are done in secrecy because they are primarily for the deceased's family.

If any family member misses out on such rites, such a member would feel s/he missed out on an important occasion to commune with "the rest of the family as well as the deceased". Some would always feel they did not complete the "funeral process". Some others would see it as an ill omen that portends evil. Some may long live to associate any future mishaps that may occur in their lives to that episode.

I served in one parish in Kenya decades of years ago. A very committed follower of one of the congregations passed on. The family came to me and together we settled for a burial date. Two days later, some other members of the family came to my house and asked me to change the day to a later date. My diary was full and changing the date was difficult. I stuck on the day we had agreed on earlier.

The family became very angry with me and to make matters worse, the elders of this congregation where the family went for worship services were siding with the family. They wanted me to change and were pressurizing the family behind my back. I found myself on one side alone.

It was later that I learned that several things were going on with this family. The deceased had spoken some unfavorable things against some members of the family and had uttered some 'curses' against some of them. The family had engaged a traditional religious leader to come and remove or break the curses before the body was buried. His one demand was that only the family members had to be there.

It was hard for this to be realized since some could not come sooner. Some lived abroad and they needed time to get there. The family was demanding that I change the date because they wanted to accommodate this new development. Usually elderly people (especially parents) are said to pronounce curses on members of the family if they mistreat, abandon, or neglect them.

The ritual of removing the "curses", locally called *kĩrumi* or in Kiswahili, *laana*, must be done before the burial takes place. Each family or clan has its own rituals that they perform before burial. This tradition is fading away slowly, but it will take a long time to die completely. The church has been at odds with it, but at times deeply embedded traditions prevail when issues as critical as death are involved. Fortunately, or unfortunately, depending on what side one is on, the new Gikuyu movement of "back to the roots" has resurrected a lot of these rites.

Commenting on the aftermath of pleasing or displeasing the spirits of the dead, Kenyatta had this to say: The Gikũyũ believe that the spirits of the dead, like living human beings, can be pleased, or displeased by the behavior of an individual or a family group, or an age-group. In order to establish a good relationship between the two worlds the ceremony of communing with the ancestral spirits is observed constantly.

The ancestral spirits can act individually or collectively. There are three main recognized groups in the spirit world:

1. The spirits of the father or mother or father (ngoma cia aciari), which communicate directly with the living children which can advise or reproach the children the same way as they did during their lifetime.
2. Clan spirits (ngoma cia muhiriga), which have an interest in the welfare and prosperity of the clan. They act collectively in accordance with the living clan, administering justice according to the behavior of the clan or any of its members;

3. Age-group spirits (ngoma cia rika). These are concerned with the activities of their particular age-group which unifies the whole tribe. It is the spirits of this group that enter into tribal affairs.[5]

The fear of reprisals from the spirits of the dead is real and there is no escape. It is, therefore, imperative that the living should make peace and do things according to the proper procedures or set order so that the departed would leave them in peace. If the departed do leave in peace, they will ensure the well-being of everyone; the family or clan and posterity will be realized.

It follows that when the spirits of the dead are happy, the living are happy and secure. The opposite is also true. If the spirits are unhappy with the living, catastrophes will befall the living. It is therefore of paramount importance that all the rituals are properly observed when someone dies so that future communion will be excellent and ascertained.

The presence of the member of the family is, therefore, vital. If the member is not present, there are doubts left as to whether everything will be all right thereafter. Kenyans living in the United States are increasingly becoming 'mourners without the body".

As the population of diaspora Kenyans increases, as their parents especially keep on aging and passing, the number of mourners without the body rises as well. Kenyan pastors are faced with the challenges arising from the complexities of dealing with this type of mourning. Some of the pastors had no prior experience of this kind of pastoral care before now, having been born and raised in communities where the

---

[5] Jomo Kenyatta, *Facing Mount Kenya; The Tribal Life of the Gikuyu* (Nairobi: Heinemann Educational Books, 1984), 146-147.

families were normally present to witness and participate in the funeral process.

Some of the pastors I have been in conversation with, decry this new phenomenon. They have numerous stories of the emotional wrecks some of the recipients are under their care. It is difficult, some aver, to replace or recreate what these mourners miss.

It is not easy especially for the young people who have come here for studies and then receive sad news of the passing on of their parents or siblings. Some are not able to travel for burial or even to support. A lot of care needs to be given to this group of mourners.

Over the years I have witnessed fundraisings for such families where those involved are helped financially to travel home for the funeral. But some cannot travel because it would be difficult if not altogether impossible for them to be allowed re-enter the country. This kind of anxiety of "one willing but cannot" drive many to near insanity.

Yes, the community is ready to assist, but it has its own limitations. One is willing to travel, but has limitations too, this makes matters worse. Imagine sending the body of a spouse or a child home to Kenya and you cannot escort it because your papers are not in order! Imagine the pain that the bereaved have to bear and the lack of closing that entail! This is hard to live with!

In summary the news of death spread like bushfire and sets things rolling. A committee is set up to oversee and organize. Religious as well as traditional rituals are set in motion. Participation of all is of great importance. If one misses out especially on the day of burial, this matter has serious repercussions for many as we shall see in the next chapter.

The Day of Burial

The day of burial is, however, the most critical. Woe betide one if s/he failed to attend a departed relative's burial especially if the dead person was a nuclear family member. As I write this paragraph, I received a call from one of our church members. She told me amidst loud wailing that her sister just lost her father-in-law. She was unable to calm her down and so was requesting me to come over and be with the family at that very sorrowful and dark time of their life.

When I talked to her sister, the first thing she said as she cried deeply and uncontrollably was that she was afraid she would not be able to travel for the funeral. She lives in one of the cities in Massachusetts and her father-in-law lives in Kenya, outside Nairobi. Her father-in-law's death was, even more painful because she lacked that close family and community support. To make matters worse, she had seen her father-in-law some ten years back. She knew of his sickness but had no chance to visit with him during the time he needed her most. Such stones like this are many.

It is difficult for one to believe that his or her loved one really died if the body is not there for them to see. Stories have been told of spouses waiting for their husbands or wives to come home even if they had been informed, they died in battle, or the sea and their remains could not be retrieved.

To view the body at the mortuary (funeral home) works like a miracle to bridge the reality of the deceased being here, yet out there. To be there on the day of the funeral helps a great deal to erase denial and to bring home reality. The communion of the living and the departed can never be greater. It is at this moment that the parting litany is said by the living. After the final goodbyes, the body is put inside a casket.

This brings about the sense that the deceased is on a journey and the mourners are escorting him/her to his/ her destination/home. The crowd of mourners, the comforting presence of the family, friends, colleagues, all standing there in support of one another, focused together and singing and "returning dust to dust", take away the fears, the anxieties, and even nabs the grief by the roots. This is not a moment for any of the bereaved member's family to miss out.

The Graveside

At the graveside, that becomes the moment of taking away all doubts. Mourners cry out, weep, moan, yell, sorrow it out. Yet, in the midst of this, they are able to let go. Each of the family members would be called forward right before the interment. The casket will be lowered into the grave. The pastor and the elders will be the first to throw in some soil as words of committal and interment are read or said orally.

The family is then invited to surround the grave and throw a handful of soil into the grave. This is done according to the order of closeness to the deceased. If married, the spouse will do it first followed by children and the parents and siblings of the deceased and so on. This is the most solemn moment of the whole funeral process. It is done in a somber mood, even in the midst of tears of love and sadness, as the family members utter

silently the solemn final words, *"Thii uhoro"*
that translates to "Rest in Peace."

The rest of the larger family would follow; then friends and close associates will have their turn. The church folk and members of the community would then have their chance, doing it alternately and sometimes simultaneously until the grave is filled with earth. All present, would make sure that they participated in shoveling back the earth into the grave.

The Kikuyu people have a saying that goes, *gũthika mũndũ ni gũikia tĩĩri* and translates into, "to bury someone is to participate in filling up the grave." The family members, relatives, and friends would then surround the grave and plant or lay flowers on top of it. This act signifies the final farewell after which the pastor would say the final prayer and benediction.

Needless to say, the funeral service is by itself a key therapy for the bereaved. The hymns, prayers, sermon, and eulogies all work together to comfort the family and to ease the final farewell that culminates at the burial site. It is a solemn moment when the religious official calls the family forward and asks them to surround the casket and then offers a prayer and a blessing to them.

This is a ritual that no family member wants to miss. It helps to connect with the deceased, and it is as if he/she were still living. The procession is also very meaningful as the family and friends get together in carrying the casket from the hearse, into and out of the church (if the dead was a church member in good standing), and to the gravesite. Everyone present, tries to make sure they rend a hand. Missing out on all these events leaves the person who neither witnesses nor participates at naught, at a loss.

If such a person is a close family member, the effect is even greater. Such is what those living abroad feel when they fail to get involved in the funerals of their loved ones. It is painful, it is devastating and at times it leads to health complications of the sufferers.

Their mourning lingers on a little longer than their counter - parts back in Kenya simply because there are no rituals that are done to help ooze it out. The testimonies of some of the members of our community who have been faced by the unavoidable choice of not being there for the funeral of their late loved ones speak for themselves.

A survey was conducted by way of a questionnaire to collect data from some of them. They responded to seventeen questions (see Appendix 1). Some were based on how they got the news, their initial reactions, how they felt knowing that they will not attend the funeral, the help they got, the nature of their mourning and the stage it reached, and finally how they can help those in similar situations.

The responses have one thing in common. The bereaved felt so bad because they could neither attend nor be physically present to participate in the funeral process. All said they have not stopped grieving and they sometimes dream their departed relatives are still alive and they will somehow meet with them sometime in the future.

The analysis of each of the responses will be given at length in the coming chapters of this book. Given one wish, all agreed they would have chosen to be there during the funeral process. They all say it would have helped them to close the grieving period and feel connected with their departed. Not doing so has left them mourning and detached and at times disconnected.

They all say they are excited about forming a therapy group in which they can share and assist each other on their way to recovery. For them, the questionnaire is integral, and they agree it can help them as a guide through the process. Perhaps it will recreate the rituals they missed and help them feel reconnected to the spirits of the persons they did not help bury.

To emphasize how critical this is, let me give a few examples. I have come across not a few members of our community carrying albums or tablets full of pictures.

They readily invite or request their friends to have a look through them. They explain almost every detail in the pictures. On most occasions, they are photographs of their deceased family members taken when they were alive, and on the day, they were buried. This could be a pointer to their lack of closure. Their grieving is still raw.

A new phenomenon is unfolding for those in the Diaspora. Most of the adults are unable to travel back. The children, however, can travel. Some have been born here and so are citizens while others have gotten papers through the dream Act (DACA) or other legal avenues. When death strikes family members of their parents, they are the ones who travel or take the body home depending on where the person passes on.

This leaves the parents in an awkward situation, being represented by their children in such critical matters, instead of the other way round. This leaves them feeling helpless if not "cornered" by circumstances. It does not help their grief. Placing such heavy responsibility on their children is uncomforting if not unsettling.

The children wouldn't understand the rites that are done during the funeral and burial of the deceased. The parents would be left feeling they have involved their children in matters that were beyond their comprehension and scope. The importance of these rituals cannot be overemphasized.

The Kikuyu people as was common with other African tribes had to consult a medicine - man or a witchdoctor for cleansing and counseling following funeral ceremonies.

These specialists, according to Mbiti, belong to the group of the medicine-men. They have had their training before they perform their duties. In their profession they also are known to be in contact with the living-dead and spirits. Medicine-men on the other hand do not necessary do that. In practice, they do interact in their roles and the "specialist" would combine the roles of medicine-man and diviner. The distinction is unclear, even hazy, and it is common to find that the names given to them are similar, one and the same.

This is what Mbiti says about them:

> The main duty of mediums is to link the human beings with the living-dead and the spirits. Through them messages are received from the other world, or the men are given knowledge of things that would otherwise be difficult or impossible to know...
>
> The medium gives information concerning the cause, nature and treatment of disease (or any other misfortune) and concerning loss thefts or loss of articles. It is then the duty of the diviner to follow or interpret the instructions from the medium.[6]

After funeral services, it was common for the family to undergo a purification rite. The medicine-man would visit with the family and guide them in the rituals necessary for cleansing so that the family could return to normal life. Such rituals included being anointed with oil that was splashed onto the family using a fly whisk. Incantations were said in prayer to the Almighty to help the family get out of the misfortune. The family would have their heads shaved clean. This was one of the most conspicuous signs of the ritual.

---

[6] Mbiti, 173

The medicine-man would be consulted on the cause of death of the deceased person. The Kikuyu believed *gũtĩrĩ ũkuaga gũtarĩ gĩtũmi* meaning no one dies without a reason. Usually this is not taken lightly. An aura of suspicion surrounded death especially if the deceased was young and energetic.

It was commonly believed that regardless of what a person died from, the person was probably bewitched, and the family had the responsibility to find out who was the culprit. If it was possible, they had to avenge the deceased by punishing the one who caused his death.

In sudden death, this was more the case, and anyone thought to be the cause was liable to heavy punishment. The family at times could enroll a witch to poison the culprit. There was a lot of witch-hunting and hate and victimization of others that went along with this. However, the family was healed if they knew the cause of death. Kenyatta has this to say about the issue of divination:

When misfortune or illness befalls a homestead (the homestead was the family with a man or woman being head of household) or a member of a family, a cause and source of the misfortune had to established. A medicine-man *(mundo-mugo)* had to be contacted, in order to ascertain the cause or the one responsible for the misfortune. It was common assumption that misfortunes were caused by spirits, singularly or plurally. The *mundu mugo* would employ divination by the casting of lots, in order to find out what particular spirit or spirits are causing the malaise and why.

When the *mũndũ-mũgo* points out the spirit(s) he proceeds then to find what reason caused it to act in such an unfriendly way; also, what the spirit would accept to appease its anger and thus restore the individual to health.

The cause of the anger may be that the family has had a feast in which they forgot the departed by not inviting them or giving them their share. In this case, if the feast in question consisted of a goat or a sheep which was killed for food, and a beer-drinking party, the same feast has to be given in a lesser degree to symbolize the one already passed. The spirits so offended would be invited to and offered food from the feast and asked to communicate with and resume friendly relations with the living family and individuals.[7]

It is important to emphasize that the communion with the dead is critical. There is no greater communion than being there at the final send-off when the deceased is embarking on the journey to the spirit world. Those unable to be present at such a time also do not usually get involved in the rituals that accompany or follow the funeral.

Unless something is done to fill that void, these people (mourners) might live with guilt all their lives. It is therefore important to devise a ritual that can fill this void and satisfy the yearnings of a heart that cries for water, but the fountain is yonder and unreachable. What relief can we offer to such mourners, just like the United Nations Relief Services offers help to those in trouble like the Haitians after being hit by a devastating calamity?

The day of burial is critical. Being present at the graveside is of paramount importance. Throwing that handful of soil into the grave is significant. Taking part in the rituals at the graveside and after the burial cannot be substituted for anything else. It is understood as escorting the dead to the

---

[7] Kenyatta, 145 - 146,

next world. The Kikuyu have a saying, *"Kumagaria mũndũ nĩ kũmũringia Mbagathi."* This means to see off someone is to escort the person to the riverbank (of Athi River) and bid them goodbye as they cross over to the other side. If one misses out, it is important that a way be found to help such a person to do so. This is the idea behind this project.

The venture was carried out in an immigrant church (real names are deliberately left out for the sake of keeping the people concerned anonymous). The church was birthed, like many others in someone's house on an Easter Sunday, 2006. A pastor from a neighboring city who the members knew, helped the group to organize. This was the same pastor who introduced me to the group.

On their first anniversary, my wife and I were the guest preachers. It was at their request that we relocated to minister with them in their city. We met with the group's leaders and consented. Within three months after our initial meeting, we joined the group, and I became their pastor.This was in the summer of 2007. We moved from the Southeast and settled in the Northeast of the country. That was quite a move, wasn't it!

The group had quite a few moves, from a hotel to a church to a hall and finally to its own property. The history of this project can be traced back to my ministry in that medium sized fellowship. This fact does not preclude my other experiences with various other immigrant communities in the New England area.

The author is a minister who gets actively involved in community affairs way beyond the four walls of any church. To come back to the point above, and to give credit where it is due, the fire that ignited within and the experiences that the author encountered in the group, quickly spread out to other areas in New England.

The reason for this latter eventuality was because

immigrants in other areas were going through similar if not parallel experiences during the same period. Further credence to the usefulness of this venture and the need for this enterprise was added. People were crying out (and still continue to) for help.

Many are groping for support. I, myself looked for it at one time and it was hard to come by. The little that I got was inadequate and uncoordinated. It was altogether lacking in quality and substance. Someone had to wake up to the challenge to come up with a tool that can be used to help the situation. I felt compelled to make an attempt. The idea to come up with this book was hatched and the rest is history.

Let me now come to the rationale of establishing the context. This is because it was the context in which the inspiration and the need to write this book was sown, watered, germinated, and sprouted, so to speak. Maybe, perhaps, maybe, if I were serving in a different setting, I'd have taken a different direction.

I was relatively new as the pastor of this small congregation and unfortunate things happened one after another in what I describe as one long year for us, myself, my family, and members of the congregation. There was a time I was wondering if this was for real, or it was one long bad dream. Unfortunately, it was real, it was not a dream and we had to live through it. That was in the year of our Lord, 2008.

Heavy Losses

During the course of the year 2008, the group suffered heavy blows in terms of losses of relatives through death back in Kenya. More than ten families were touched by these unfortunate tragedies, sometimes more than once. The deaths had heavy impact on the lives of the families and by extension, the fellowship.

My family was not spared either. We lost a few people, the most important of all, my own biological father. The group was wailing, it was crying, it was moaning, it was grieving, and it continued to mourn. The scourge continued to the next year and the next. In the subsequent year alone, we lost five more under similar circumstances.

The group was not alone. In other cities the same was happening. The community was losing more and more relatives in Kenya and here in the Diaspora. This unfortunately is a phenomenon we are learning the hard way to live with. This additional aspect made me pick my pen and start compiling what constitutes this book. Thanks to the group I was doing ministry with.

The Kikuyu Community

The members of the church I was ministering belonged to the same tribe back in Kenya, the Kikuyu. Occasionally, an individual, a family, or a small group of people from other ethnic groups in Kenya or another African country would visit, express desire to be part of the church, but somehow, for unexplained reasons none stuck to the group. They would slowly drift away.

The Kikuyu group of peoples has very strong ties to their families, clan, and communities. Even when some members move abroad, the ties are not broken. They are even made stronger because the family, clan and community still remember and miss those of their own who have moved to different locations.

These family units come together in times of celebrating their successes as well as in times of loss. The most significant of such times is during the passing on of one of its members. During such occasions everyone is expected to be present to participate in the funeral process and what goes on in it. The philosophy behind this is to give all an opportunity to grief and mourn together with the others, a process that has over time proved to be very effective.

Unfortunately, it is not always the case. Due to the high mobility of people in our present world, some relatives miss out to bury their dead for a variety of reasons. No city, church or community enjoy an exception. There are times when some members are not able to travel and so mourn and grief in isolation, without the body.

As stated earlier, several families have been victims and hence the reason for writing this project is validated. How to step in and assist each other in the grieving and mourning with an aim to growth toward healing is at the heart of this project. The specific goal is to seek to help the community to first identify and express their grief. How do we answer the cry, "I am hurting?" How do we help those who are groping for support?

Some answers and suggestions will be provided. Secondary to that, the author, has chosen to employ the western therapeutic model of pastoral care giving as far much as is practically possible to lead the affected people (members) to wholeness.

An inter-play of both models is important because of the peculiar circumstances the members live in. A clear explanation of this argument follows in the next chapter. The chapter gives a flashback to the past and the reason why both methods are useful in order to be as helpful to those suffering/grieving as much as possible.

4

Death, Theology, and the Church

Is there a connection between death, theology, and the church? Is our understanding of death informed by our understanding of God? What has the church to do with it? What is the church's role in reconciling the two? Perhaps it is important to talk about the three before we commence on the events that took place in trying to help the group that came together to seek support after their losses.

The passing of a loved one is never sought for. It comes with regrets to those attached to the deceased. Even in cases of sickness where the loved one is in real pain and wishes to pass on, it is never easy for the family to let go. If the family must, the decision comes slowly and with a lot of misgivings. Sometimes it takes the doctors and counselors and chaplains to convince the family that their patient has almost next to zero chance of survival. The author has been involved in such scenarios and they have not been easy.

At times the family is divided over the issue of withdrawing care, and they haggle over it, until desperation takes the better part, unwillingly and with a lot of hesitation, they see no hope and having nothing else to hold onto, they hesitatingly let go. It is a choice taken more by compulsion rather than out of one's own volition. It's hard, but if there is no other way, then it becomes that proverbial bitter pill to swallow. It is like they say, "When you hit bottom, there is only one way to go, up."

But, when death occurs because of an accident, suddenly from heart attacks, strokes, or other natural calamities, it is a different matter altogether. The family and other close people to the victim of such circumstances are left devastated and if care, support, and other forms of assistance are not provided, possible dire consequences on the bereaved folk can be expected.

It is on this premise that we are each other's keeper and that our theological argument fronted in this book has a footing. God gives us a heart to empathize, love and care. He works in us as we provide and give the same to those in need. And this gives further credence to our theological rationale.

Under normal circumstances, when human beings die, they are given a decent burial. How people treat their dead can be used as a measure of how they value life. Some of the most conspicuous landmarks of our cities are cemeteries. In almost all cases, they are well cared for and looking from the outside, they are good sights.

Funeral homes are spread all over our cities and they look well kept, too. The practice of taking dead bodies inside beautiful and expensive caskets to church is an old ecclesiastical tradition. Some of the most exquisite cars are hearses. What is their purpose other than transporting dead bodies to their final resting ground, the grave?

Except in the movies, in normal life, dead bodies are treated with respect and honor. In all societies and religions, I know, during the paying of the last respects to a departed soul, and especially the funeral services, a religious leader, priest, pastor, imam, Jain, Caliph, Guru, etc. are involved and they lead the service.

Death and the ensuing process of mourning and disposing of the body has had a theological side to it. The church has been very active in this area. Part of the understanding of ourselves has to do with what death means to us.

Memorial and funeral services are common features in our church bulletins and weekly newsletters. Most hospitals in this country have chaplaincy/spiritual services departments where bereaved families can seek pastoral, emotional and spiritual care within the hospital environment where incidentally a lot of people pass on. But then, that is where we rush our people when they are in a critical and life-threatening condition.

Life is Inter-related

Human beings are social beings and are interrelated and interdependent. The couples, family, neighborhood, church, community, and many more are all examples of human units. Where relations are healthy, the demise of a member of these units has effects on those who are left behind.

In varying degrees and/or measures, the bereaved grieve over the departed. The intensity of grief increases with how close the one grieving is to the deceased person. The closer the relationship to the deceased the more the weight resulting from her/his demise.

J. William Worden has this to say in his book, Grief Counseling and Grief Therapy:

> Before one can fully comprehend the impact
> of a loss and the human behavior associated
> with it, one must have some understanding

of attachment. There is considerable writing in the psychological and psychiatric literature as to the nature of attachments--- what they are and how they develop. One of the key figures and primary thinkers in this area is the late British psychiatrist, John Bowlby. He devoted much of his professional career to the area of attachment and loss and wrote several substantial volumes as well as a number of articles on the subject... [8]

When the goal of attachment behavior is to maintain an affection bond, situations that endanger this bond give rise to certain specific reactions. The greater the potential loss, the more intense these reactions and the more varied. "In such circumstances, all the most powerful forms of attachment behavior become activated--clinging, crying, and perhaps angry coercion...when these actions are successful, the bond is restored, the activities cease and the states of stress and distress are alleviated (Bowlby, 1977, p. 42). If the danger is not removed, withdrawal, apathy and despair ensue. [9]

Close attachments are likely to result in greater pain when death curtails them and suddenly brings them to a halt or to an end. The degree of the intensity of grief resulting from such severances can sometimes have far reaching effects especially if one is mourning in isolation or in exclusion of others.

---

[8] William Worden; Grief Counseling and Grief Therapy: (NY: Spring Publishing Company, 2002), 7.
[9] Ibid., 8

Experience has proven that grief is likely to ebb faster if it is "shared grief" and especially if it is shared between close and familiar people. If the conditions are right, people who share the same blood normally work through grief better and faster than people who are strangers. This is simply because the closer people are, the more they have in common.

This is by extension and theologically true of those who share in the same blood of the Son of God. Those who are related thus can help each other in handling their grief when calamity strikes. Our denominations, our Christian fellowships and other faith communities usually become cities of refuge whenever we are walking in the valley of the shadow of death.

What binds us in faith also helps when we need support especially when our base is shaken. With the crumbling of families, the alternative that seems to work best is the community that arises from what we have in common. Such are communities of interest, and perhaps the strongest amongst them are our communities of faith.

In these communities, we get help that we cannot find anywhere else. Most of the help is free and valuable. It is only in such communities that our hearts are spoken to and touched and healed and still in the same communities our healing hearts have space to reach out and touch other hearts.

Grief therapy groups will perhaps work best where the participants share the same faith. Increased connection is likely better achieved in a group where people share almost similar perceptions, attitudes, beliefs and perspectives about the meanings of life and death.

Grieving in isolation can be devastating. I have personally experienced it. I have also witnessed its negative effects on members of the churches I have served. The churches are largely made up of Kenyan immigrants living in the United States in general but in the New England area in particular.

I vividly remember that dark period in my life. It was deplorable and hard on me. My dad passed away in Kenya in very unprecedented and untimely circumstances. This added to the long list of other community members who had similar losses.

Here is what happened: During the week of January 19 through 24, 2010 three families lost their loved ones back in Kenya. This was in addition to the number of several others who lost one or more family members the previous couple of years. Some of those who had been bereaved were single individuals and some were families, but mostly it is the individual who is closest to the deceased who is most hit by the tsunami that we call death and therefore suffers more than the others.

Matters are not made any better by the fact that most of the bereaved are unable or are not able to travel to Kenya to mourn with the family, the clan and the community. The individual(s) is left to mourn and grieve alone, far from their relatives and therefore rarely does grief become "shared grief."

The mourners stand the chance of suffering from "withdrawal, apathy and despair," as Bolden has stated in the paragraph above, if no intervention is initiated or forthcoming, those who are unable to participate in the funeral process of their loved ones, suffer a double loss.

First, they do not see the body of the departed; second, they do not participate in bidding the body goodbye or in the rituals, before and after. In an earlier chapter, funeral rites and rituals are discussed in depth to show how important one's presence is during the funeral and burial process of a loved one. All that brings us to the main goal of this book: How to assist the grieving without the body and those related to them.

In other words, the focus is on how to help a bereaved

person to grieve when the body is neither there, nor somewhere near. How can we reach out and hold their outstretched arm that is groping for support? In this book some ways in which we can be supportive will be suggested and discussed.

Jesus' Mandate

Helping and supporting those in grief is an act of ministry, which we belong to. If this ministry is neglected, it is possible we will have a community full of walking zombies. There is a saying that goes, "We are not free until everyone is free". The well-being of each person impacts on the well-being of us all. If one of us is bleeding from grief, it follows that we are all bleeding. If one of us suffers loss, we are in a way also affected by the loss.

Apart from preaching the good news, the primary responsibility of the church is to take care of the needs of its members and primarily, those who are in any kind of suffering or distress. When Jesus first preached, he quoted from Isaiah 61: 1-2 and using these words from Isaiah, he set his mission agenda.

In Luke 4, we read:

> "The Spirit of the Lord is on me, because he has anointed me to preach good news to the poor. He has sent me to proclaim freedom for the prisoners and recovery of sight for the blind, to release the oppressed; to proclaim the year of the Lords' favor" (NIV Bible Luke 4:18-19.)

The Spirit of the church is the spirit of Jesus. The church is the body of Christ and thus performs and executes the work of Christ. The mandate of Christ stated above is the mandate of the church. Those who are mourning are like any sufferer from any other malady. Suffering is not one sided. It is multifaceted and comes in many forms.

The mourning and the grieving need to hear the good news. They need someone to tell them God still cares, loves them and He has good plans for them. Jeremiah had these encouraging words for the grieving exiles that had been forcibly transplanted from their land in Jerusalem to Babylon and were grieving the loss of family connections, the land, and the Temple: This is what the Lord says:

> "When seventy years are completed for Babylon, I will come to you and fulfill my gracious promise to bring you back to this place. For I know the plans I have for you," declares the Lord, "plans to prosper you and not to harm you, plans to give you hope and a future. Then you will call upon me and come and pray to me, and I will listen to you. You will seek me and find me when you seek me with all your heart. I will be found by you," declares the Lord, "and will bring you back from captivity. I will gather you from all the nations and places I have banished you," declares the Lord, "and will bring you back to the place from which I carried you into exile" (NIV, Jer. 29:10-14).

This promise in Jeremiah is a promise for all time because God's word remains fresh and true across the generations. It is applicable to those who are in similar physical, spiritual, emotional, social, or psychological situations right now. Mourning over loss is the same in all situations. The church has a wealth of resource in God's word and God has given her the divine responsibility of using and interpreting this resource to encourage, to comfort, and to bring hope and assurance to God's people.

Those who mourn are not unlike the poor in spirit. They are not unlike those imprisoned in the prisons of worry, grief and anxiety. They are in a position of oppression, mental or otherwise and need someone to proclaim to them the good news that God is still at work and that their Jubilee is nigh and at hand.

They need to hear that God will restore them, care for them, and replace their loss with peace and acceptance and give them hope and a future. They need to hear that all is not lost and that the Lord of the living also reigns over the spirits of the dead, and that in Christ they live in God's nearer presence.

Some of the most inviting and hopeful places in the New Testament that echo the promise in Jeremiah 29 above, are Jesus' words in Matthew 7:7: "Ask and it will be given to you; seek and you will find; knock and the door will be opened to you". Matthew also records Jesus' open invitation to those in distress: "Come to me all of you who are weary and burdened, and I will give you rest" (NIV, Matt. 11:28).

Surely, the mourning and grieving have a heavy burden, a burden that calls for relief. The Word of God and the work of God in us offers the best and long-lasting relief and release anyone can and will ever get. As a recap of this argument, God gave the first ordained clergy (Aaron, the brother of Moses) a charge to pronounce God's benediction over God's people by lifting up his hands and saying these words: "The Lord God bless you and keep you; The Lord make his face shine upon you and be gracious to you; the Lord turn his face toward you and give you peace" (NIV Num. 6:22ff).

What beautiful words to those in grief! The church is

entrusted in passing and dispensing these oracles to God's people. It is on this basis that our foundation for engaging ourselves in associating, helping, and standing with those cumbered with pain, loss and grief is founded.

The Bible continues to encourage us to mourn with those who are mourning (Eccl. 7: 1ff). It becomes comes clear to us that it is better to go to a house of mourning than a house of feasting. The reason behind this argument is that in a house of mourning, we are reminded of our common destiny.

The way I understand it is that Jesus wants us to see the need to stand with one another as we are all together walking down the same rough road. Only time separates us from each other's turn to mourn. Each one has her/his day. None of us is immune to suffering. None of us is spared the ordeal. At some point in our lives, we'll have to face it, live it, experience it and deal with it.

Jesus as an Example

Jesus himself grieved with those whose loved ones passed on during his physical presence in Palestine. The death of Lazarus is one of our best examples (John 11:13). Lazarus lived in Bethany with his two sibling sisters, Martha, and Mary. They occasionally invited Jesus to visit with them. They were close friends with Jesus.

One day Lazarus fell seriously sick and was at the point of death. Mary and Martha sent out someone to tell Jesus the bad news of his friend and their brother, Lazarus. Though the message called for immediate action and response, it did not seem like an emergency to Jesus. I think it was because Jesus had confidence he could reverse the situation; life to death and back to life again. He tarried before he showed up at Lazarus' home.

When Jesus got there, he found Lazarus had been buried in a tomb four days prior to his arrival. His showing up seemed to be of no consequence and even Mary told him something like, "if you had been here, my brother would not have died" (John 11:21, NIV). But she ended up by sounding hopeful, "But, I know that even now God will give you whatever you ask" (John 11:22, NIV). Jesus assured her that her brother would rise again.

She ran back to the house and told Mary, her sister, about the presence of Jesus. Mary came out mourning and when Jesus beheld her condition, he was deeply moved and empathizing with her, he too wept. It was at that point that Jesus declared himself as the author of life and the resurrection; He that gives life even when it is taken away.

He demonstrated what he meant by bringing Lazarus back to life after he had been buried for over four days. He restored happiness and joy to the grieving family and all the mourners who were there. Above all, his presence, his encouraging words, his weeping with the family, the healing and hope he brought to the mourners created a perfect example of what the role of the church in such circumstances should be.

The church should go out and meet the mourners where they are. Jesus dealt with the family one on one, first with Martha, then Mary and finally with the rest of the mourners. He expressed his feelings openly and walked down the road of grief with them. He held their groping hand, so to speak.

At the tomb, the seemingly end of the road, he brought resurrection and hope. He restored what had been lost. The church by declaring Jesus' promises can help rekindle the fragile and broken hearts and hopes of the mourning. In his words about life and resurrection, Jesus implies that death is not the end of life. There's hope beyond death, and in this belief, our greatest encouragement lies.

The story about the death and resurrection of Jesus gives

mankind, and particularly the believers in Christ, the best hope ever seen in this universe. According to the accounts in the Gospel stories, Jesus was arrested during the Passover, most likely on a Thursday night. He was rushed through trial before both religious and secular rulers of the day. The Temple rulers, the Sanhedrin, found him guilty.

Amazingly and to the contrary, neither of the two secular rulers before whom he appeared, Pontius Pilate and Herod, found any evidence that he was in violation of any of the laws of the land. They said so candidly before the religious rulers, but it did not work to Jesus' advantage. The religious rulers used trumped up serious charges against Jesus, the most serious of all being he claimed he was God and thus blasphemed against God.

Blasphemy was the most serious offense / sin any Jew could commit and was punishable by nothing short of death. When this charge did not hold, they incited the crowds who shouted and cried and bayed for Jesus' life. Even when Pilate gave them an alternative to releasing Jesus and keeping a dangerous criminal who was due for pardon behind bars longer, they declined this logical offer and begged for Jesus' blood.

They declined Pilate's offer to release Jesus and opted for the release of Barabbas. Pilate reluctantly granted their request but not before he washed his hands of the case. He did not want to go against the wishes of the Sanhedrin lest they give a bad report about him to Caesar, the Roman emperor, his boss and antagonist. There was bad blood between the two.

To please the Jews and to win them over to his side, he sacrificed the life of an innocent man. Although he had declared three times in front of many witnesses that he found not an iota of any faulty incrimination, he became a prey to the wishes of the crowd. When the Jews demanded for Jesus to be punished, he granted their wish. He went against his good sense and verdict in favor of Jesus and handed him (Jesus) into their hands to be killed.

The trial was a prolonged process and because Jesus was popular with the people and commanded a sizeable following, as many people had turned up for the hearing. Incidentally, maybe by design, not one of his disciples was called to testify in his defense. The rank and file under the incitement of the religious leaders had their day. Jesus had to die.

The hopes of his genuine followers who had hoped somehow their leader and master would be released for lack of evidence had waned. Their hope was dashed against a hard wall when Pilate declared his verdict. Pilate had him whipped, then handed over to his accusers to finish with him. The trial was a sham and a big example of mockery of justice. It was one-sided, hurried, and full of holes considering the evidence presented.

It stands out as one of the most unfair, biased and discriminatory trial in all history. Their one desire was to eliminate him. He had challenged and disturbed the status quo. The religious super class felt threatened by his mere presence. He could move masses just by his being present. They came out and followed him in droves when they heard he was in town. The Pharisees and Sadducees though they differed in some theological perspectives, on this issue, they were of one resolve: Jesus had to go, period!

Though they had no genuine reasons to charge him, they dragged him before both religious and secular courts for trial. They brought up trumped up charges against him. To circumvent justice and to put pressure on the secular leader, Pontius Pilate, after threatening him, they hyped up the emotions of mobs to near riot. Pilate, fearing to be reported to Caesar (his emperor boss), and dreading the rowdy mobs, surrendered to the evil plot of the religious rulers (the Sanhedrin), and succumbed to the insincere will of the mob in order to restore peace. Jesus became the victim of their ire. That cost him his innocent life.

Sticking Together

According to Mark, amongst the group that witnessed Jesus' execution were his mother, Mary Magdalene, Mary the mother of James and Salome amongst many others, including his disciples and close confidants, the eleven (Judas had already left and was perhaps dead by now). Of that group, three women, Mary Magdalene, Mary the mother of James and Salome are significant in that they were the first witnesses of the resurrection.

After following Jesus through his trial, his undeserved punishment and crucifixion, they perhaps had hoped, that his body would be given to one of his disciples or family to go and bury, but it was not to be the case unfortunately. By the time Jesus died and was pulled down from the cross, it was nearing evening and time for the start of the Sabbath. It was Friday evening and Sabbath observation was close.

It was therefore in a hurry that Joseph of Arimathea, a member of the Temple council, but Jesus' secret follower, requested for Jesus' body from Pilate. His request was granted, and he got the body and had it buried in his own (Joseph's) grave prepared before his own death. Perhaps the women followed those who buried Jesus, saw where they put the body and then rushed home in time for Sabbath.

They had to rush before the same law that was applied to put Jesus to death was applied on them. It was unlawful to walk on the Sabbath for a distance longer than the law permitted. Sabbath began at sundown on a Friday and ended at the same time on Saturday. The women, whether they liked it or not, had to stay home, unless they were bold enough to ask for trouble. These poor women, shocked, grief stricken, emotionally wrecked, hopeless, and helpless trudged home crestfallen and in tears that Friday evening.

If we were to speculate on what happened that day, we may conclude that these women had seen Jesus' collapse from afar. They saw his lifeless body given to a man they might not have known for whatever reasons. Curious of what they intended to do with Jesus' body, the women followed them (those who carried Jesus to the grave) or gathered information about where they disposed of the body.

They knew it was in a grave because they bought and brought perfumes to anoint the body. They did not participate in the burial of Jesus. They also did not get involved in the rituals that followed the death of a family member, a relative or a friend. They did not get a chance to say goodbye to the one they loved so much. They were in a sense grieving without the body.

The Sabbath must have been long, anxious, and tormenting. They could not wait for it to end.

Common sense makes one think they went to a cosmetics store and bought some spices with which to anoint Jesus' body. They huddled together that Friday night, mourning, crying, grieving and trying to comfort each other. The next morning, very early that morning before daybreak, they got out and walked, perhaps running toward the place where they saw Jesus buried.

On the way they wondered and asked of each other who would help them roll away the stone that they perhaps had seen, or thought was used to secure the entrance into the grave. They were unsure whether they would find access into the grave to see the body and anoint it, but their faith and love in Jesus kept them going.

When they got there, they could not believe it. The stone had been rolled away. The body of Jesus was nowhere to be found. Their grief was further exacerbated and maybe became too much to handle. They were all groping for help. Luckily an angel (a young man in white) was present, and he supplied the support and presence they so desperately needed at that hour.

They were advised not to look for the living amongst the dead. They pleaded with the man to tell them where he had taken the body so that they might pay Jesus the last respects. But the angel told them the good news that Christ had risen. They should take the good news to the disciples and tell them Christ will meet them in Galilee as he had promised.

The women desired to give to Jesus a decent burial. They wanted to see, touch, and anoint his body. They desired to perform the ritual of anointing the body, perhaps crying over it and saying goodbye. That would have been a beginning of a journey towards healing. Their grief would have been cut by a large extent, their broken hearts would have been comforted, they would have found a bit of some reprieve and peace. It was that kind of peace that Mary Magdalene found when Jesus first made his first post resurrection appearance to her, according to Mark. (Mark 16:9ff).

In comparison to some cases of bereavement, these women were lucky. Unlike most other people, they at least saw Jesus collapse on the cross, though definitely from afar. Some people never get the chance to see their people pass on. They only get to hear about it much to their disbelief and shock. Still, some of these people do not participate in the burial of their loved ones. They miss out on almost everything including the vital part of the rituals that accompany the funeral process.

If these women were deeply disturbed and troubled before early that Sunday morning, and had to go to great lengths to see the body, how then are those who have no hope of seeing the bodies of their loved ones forever? If there was no chance, ever to see their loved ones, what can be done to help them meet the challenges that come with grief?

How can the same Jesus who took away grief from those women help these unfortunate ones to deal with the ordeal of grief? How can they in turn go out and reach others and tell them that in grief, there is hope, and in Christ there is healing? This is the bedrock of what we want to achieve at the end of this venture.

This narrative about the three women is one of the stories that clearly show the intensity of grief and the hopelessness that follows. It points to the fact that someone should come to help and offer support to persons who are grieving. "Who will roll away the stone?" Someone should help! This shows ultimately that only God who works from the inside of us can really take away grief that bogs us down when we become victims.

Our God as Paul puts it is "the Father of compassion and the God of all comfort" (2 Cor. 1:3f). One can at times wonder what would have happened if the three women did not stick and mourn together. If they did not, would any one of them have gone to the grave that early Sunday morning? It is on this basis that we hold it to be true that together we can walk down the "road of grief' and together with our Lord, we will emerge victorious on the other side spreading out the news that there is hope and life after grief. This model can be very useful for churches to implement walking together, holding that groping hand, supporting one another.

It is important to mention how the disciples of Jesus grieved. When their master died on the cross and before their very eyes, they left and went back to their shared abode (the upper room). They stayed together for several days, crying, mourning, and grieving the loss of their friend, teacher and hope. They must have been comforting each other and giving each other encouragement as they reminisced on the life and words of their master.

While there, the good news came to them that Christ was alive. Though some doubted, they all had their hearts healed and soon had to hit the road with the good news of the risen Lord. One of the disciples, Thomas, was not with them when the Lord first appeared to them. He could not believe Jesus had risen unless he saw and felt the body of The Risen Jesus (John 20: 24-28). He was in great doubts of the new reality. He needed a physical ritual to see, touch and feel to believe. Such I think is what happens when many people are not there to witness, to see and to feel when their family member passes on. For those who are visual, the problem is even more compounded.

Still Some More

The Old Testament is also replete with mourning families and individuals: the death of Jacob in Egypt (Gen. 50: 1-22) and that of Joseph (Gen. 50: 23-26); the death of Absalom, a beloved son of David (2 Sam.18: 9-33), and of his son with Bathsheba (2 Sam. 12: 15b-23).

Another sad story in the Old Testament is that of the death of Eli's two sons in battle and of his own sudden death, when the shock from the news about their deaths overwhelmed him and shock and grief sent him to his own grave (1 Sam. 4: 12-18). He died even before he saw their bodies. The shock from the news got the better of him and sealed his fate. In all these cases, grief is apparent. Support was necessary. All of them look like overwhelming situations.

The story of Job has been used over the centuries to console those suffering from loss. This ranges from the spouse who now wishes he/she would curse God and die, to the loss of property, animals, friends and many more. Job suffered many woes, but I think the death of his children was the most devastating. Instead of him getting comfort and encouragement from his friends, they accused him of being the source of his own misfortune.

They constantly intimate that his suffering is as a result of his sin, and he is the cause of his own curse. Those were Job's four friends, Elihu, Eliphaz, Bildad and Zophar.

Together they tried to make the case that Job's suffering was because of his own doing. And that God was punishing him because of his own sin, though he was by far a very righteous man by any standard. However, Job somehow got some comfort from his friends.

They mourned with him, cried, and talked with him about faith. They gave him some support as far as presence and companionship is concerned. They led him to re-examine his walk with God. He also had opportunity to search his own heart and finally he encountered God and his healing was realized. He was paid double of what he had lost (whatever that means), and it is my hunch that he realized double strength in overcoming his grief.

The New Testament also contains similar accounts. Paul encourages Christians to comfort those who are in any kind of trouble (2 Cor. 1:3-8) and to mourn with those who mourn (Romans 12:15). The Bible also promises comfort to those in grief and are mournful. Echoes of Jeremiah 31:13 (Old Testament) that there is a promise that God will restore God's people and "turn their mourning to gladness" are to be found in the New Testament.

The last book in the Bible, Revelation 21: 4, points us to the hope of the end of grief and mourning at the close of age. Chapter 22 creates a beautiful picture of the healing of nations at the return of Christ. All this proves the fulfillment of Jesus' agenda as set out in Luke 4:16ff. In John 10:10b,

Jesus states the purpose of his coming and that is for us to enjoy life in its fullness. Does fullness not include happiness, good health, joy, and wholeness amongst other things!

Since some of those mourning and grieving people (members) are in the church, this becomes a ministry that should be given much attention as everything else if not greater. When they (members) are suffering, the church is suffering.

The effect of their suffering has significant impact on the congregation. Grief affects the spiritual, psychological, emotional and physical wellbeing of the victim. Its grip on a person speaks volumes of ramifications on the victim and in most cases; the homeostasis of a person is thrown into disarray. The church as a place of healing needs to address and offer help and support to such people.

Jesus is the healer. The church is his body. When the body is ill, Jesus also suffers with it. When any part of the body suffers, all the other parts suffer because all the parts are interconnected and can never be separated. No part is dispensable, and no part can stand aloof and say it does not care about the other parts and can do it of its own. When a finger hurts, the whole body hurts. Even the eye that seems to perform a very different function in comparison to the finger sheds tears in sympathy.

The pastor is a co-worker with Christ. It is therefore the pastor's task to ensure that the sheep (congregation) are given the best shepherding possible. The health of the congregation should be the primary focus of the pastor. When an individual grieves, the pastor normally grieves with him or her. A sick church is counterproductive.

The Westminster Catechism has this to say about the chief end of humanity: "The chief end of man is to glorify God and enjoy him forever". The question then arises: How can we enjoy God when we are grieving and mourning at the same time? God's will is to finally end our grief and we should co-operate, participate and work with God towards the achievement of that goal. The death, the resurrection, and the return of Christ (Parousia) all open avenues to the hope of the coming to an end of any form of suffering. This is an appeasement Christians hold dearly and look forward to. This should be the goal of our care, to move people from a condition of grief to one of hope and healing.

Personally, this endeavor accords me a chance for personal growth as well as knowledge. I have been there and continuing to mourn the loss of my father. I was not able to travel to Kenya to be with my mother, siblings, and others in the funeral and burial process. I did not have a chance to do the rites neither did I participate in the process apart from sending out some financial assistance.

I must confess that I have not even been able to muster up the courage to view the photos and videos taken on the day of the funeral. I have been there myself and so have many others within and without the church. This process will be helpful to me as I also deal with my own loss and grief.

Together we shall "share our grief" and experiences and it is my sincere hope that we shall emerge stronger and healthier than when we began. Although this seems like a parallel process, I will focus more on the ones who have lost their loved ones and make the burden to document the process so that it becomes of help to those who are or will be suffering the same fate. It was through this process of supporting one another that this book was birthed.

As the number of immigrants increases abroad, the greater is the number of people who will experience and tread the same path. A week never passes without the news of another death. Fortunately, in these our days, news spreads as fast as lightning. It only requires the click of a mouse and information will be dispersed to all those whose e-mail addresses or groups or contacts etc. were under "Send" before the mouse was clicked. This message is then forwarded to the rest and in a short time the news is all around. Cell phone calling and text messaging coupled with other technological means of communication that are present in our modern world, like; Tweeter, Facebook, WhatsApp, Instagram, and various other forms of messaging add to the phenomenon of how quickly we can convey information. The increasing number justifies the urgency of writing this book. My hope is that out of it, a chance, opportunity, or avenue will be developed for many to say the final goodbyes to their loved ones.

I am sure, there are some people who are in the situation we are talking about right now. There is always someone. There are many others who anticipate with fear and anxiety that it is in the offing sooner or later. The advantage of having a tool handy that can be used in "supporting" the groping hearts cannot be overstated.

As we continue, I will offer a brief look into some of the key sources of information that I used. Apart from giving us a background to understanding the problem and significance of supporting the grieving, it will also serve as an incentive for further reading of these and other sources for those who would like to know and learn more.

Some Helpful Sources

In my research I found the following authors amongst many others very useful. The authors helped me to understand broadly what others have said about some of the pertinent issues that were circling in my mind looking for answers. My suggestion is that for better understanding of the whole picture, the reader should read what some of these authors had to say.

I find it not redundant to say again that the broad purpose of this project was to seek ways of helping and offering pastoral support to the church and the community. I have served some who suffered the loss of their loved ones in the New England area, by helping them in devising way to go through their "grief and mourning without the body". My major goal has been to seek to help the affected to identify and to express their grief.

This would be followed by the initiation of a therapeutic process geared towards healing and ending with a document that will be helpful to others who are facing or will suffer similar fates in the future. The therapeutic process will be coupled by the common way of mourning that has been practiced for generations by the Kikuyu people.

Until recently, mourning has been a public expression, but it is slowly being converted into a private enterprise. This later development has brought with it its own emotional and spiritual deficiencies. The battle of mourning has been turned inwards other than outwards. The fire burns internally other than externally.

The internal damage has been more telling and its manifestation is evidence of grave destruction that manifests itself in many ways: anger, stress, depression, suicide, aloofness, social distress and many more. An attempt was done in this venture to employ some of the traditional methods and test whether; they are still relevant and can be useful if applied in a church setting.

Referred to below is Grief among Animals by James William Worden.

James William Worden claims that it is not just human beings who mourn. Worden cites from the work of Lorenz with animals and that of Harlow's with young monkeys as reported in Bowlby's thesis (1977). Bowlby concludes that attachment occurs even without biogenic needs that drives most of our actions and those of other animals.

Worden commenting on this statement writes:

> Bowlby's (1977) thesis, which claimed that these attachments come from a need for security and safety. They develop early in life and are usually directed toward a few specific individuals. They tend to endure throughout a large part of the life cycle. Forming attachments

is considered normal behavior not only to the child but also to the adult as well. [10]

Bowlby argues that attachment behavior has survival value, citing the occurrence of this behavior in the young of almost all species of mammals. But he sees attachment behavior as distinct from feeding and sexual behavior.

Worden goes further to explain about this attachment behavior, and he argues that, this truth is illustrated by young ones who leave their families when they are of age. They always come back to the attachment figure when they feel threatened and need support or safety. Strong anxiety and emotional stress strikes when the attachment figure disappears. This new insight came to me as I read through Worden's thesis.

If in fact even other mammals mourn the loss of their attachment figures and are so affected that they sometimes mourn themselves to death, how about human beings who have more areas of "affection" bonds (to use Worden's word) than mammals!

Worden also quotes from Charles Darwin's book, The Expressions of the Emotions in Man and Animals,[11] and describes ways in which sorrow is expressed by old and young alike, be they animals or human beings. His emphases are in the fact that grief has a way of spreading from the individual to the group. This proves the importance of this project developing to another dimension.

This also sheds light as to the importance and influence of attachments. Attachments are not severed by distance and

---

[10] William J Worden, *Grief Counseling and Grief Therapy,* Third Edition: A Handbook for the Mental Health Practitioner (NY: Springer Publishing Company, 2002), 7-8.

[11] Ibid. Worden explains, Darwin's Theory of Similarity Between Human and Animal Emotions. (Darwin, 1872).

so when losses occur, most other factors do not count. What matters most is that attachment which has been affected. How to keep it from adversely affecting the sufferer is what Worden attempts to bring out in his book. This is an important resource for informing the direction and substance of this book.

In addition, Worden is helpful in that he has a whole chapter dealing with how the counselor him/herself can handle his/her own grief. He ends his book with a chapter on how to train counselors and offers numerous case studies for that purpose; we could not have a better book!

The Bible

The Bible is one of our most important resources in this regard. The word of God calls us to "mourn with those who mourn" (Roman 12:15, NIV). In Ecclesiastes 7:2 (NIV), the wisdom writer advises: "it is better to go to a house of mourning than to go to a house of feasting."

There is power in the word of God. The word of God can be used to perform several functions that include: to bring salvation to us, to rescue us, to comfort and to encourage us, to rekindle or renew our souls. The Spirit works through the word and makes it real to us. Through the word, God communicates His message and in God's mysterious ways we come to know God and to hear God speak to our circumstances.

God has also mandated His people to work with Him even as He fulfills His purposes for humanity and to each one of us individually. It is a divine duty for the church to restore the fallen, the weary, the heavy-laden, the depressed, and the battle worn in all situations to a state of "normalcy".

The biblical stories of David mourning his son, Job

mourning his sons and daughters and his other losses, Eli mourning his sons killed in battle, the death of Lazarus, the death of Jesus and how His disciples mourned Him, are among many other forms of mourning, that form the core of the theological basis of this book.

> The context in which this project took place in the churches I have been pastoring in the Commonwealth State of Massachusetts, involved catering for and attending to the whole person. It employed holistic approach to caregiving. This was largely pastoral and involved aspects of both grief counseling and grief therapy. The physical, the spiritual and the psychological dimensions to healing were applied as necessity demanded.

J. William Worden

> In his book, *Grief Counseling and Grief Therapy*, James William Worden emphasizes the importance of "care to bereavement as a very complex issue. People experience their grief in many varied ways".[12] He says that of all the patients who passed through the mental health clinics in Massachusetts and California, 10-15 percent and 17 percent respectively had unresolved grief. He also states that research has proven that grief has significant impact on morbidity and mortality. "Grief exacerbates not only physical morbidity but psychiatric morbidity as well." [13]

[12] Ibid, 4.
[13] Ibid, 2 .

James traces how people have dealt with grief over the ages stating that close families and communities provided the mechanisms of helping the grieving. But with the disintegration of both over time, the grieving lack immediate support when death strikes. These days, people turn to the healthcare system and the church for support. This latter element is at the very heart of this book. James makes a very interesting and important observation that gives me the reason for relying on his book.

Grief has been compared to physical illness. In the Old Testament, the prophet Isaiah, 61: 1 admonishes us to bind up the broken hearted, giving the impression that severe grief can somehow do damage to the heart. Both grief and physical illness can take time for healing and, indeed, both of them include emotional and physical aspects.

In comparing physical illness and grief, social worker Bertha Simos made this observation:

Both may be self-limiting or require intervention by others. And in both, recovery can range from a complete return to the pre-existing state of health and well-being, to the partial recovery, to improved growth and creativity, or both can inflict permanent damage, progressive decline, and even death (Simos, 1979, p. 30).14

Worden sees grief from a two-pronged perspective. He sees it as having both emotional and physical aspects. He sees grief as a disease and argues that "the loss of a loved one is psychologically traumatic to the same extent as being severely wounded or burned is physiologically traumatic".

He states that grief represents a departure from the state of health and well-being. It requires sometimes for return to normal status. Just like a physiological malady requires some time to heal, psychological distress requires the same. Just as medication and other forms of therapies are needed for remedying sickness, pastoral intervention is needed to counteract the effect of grief.

Worden also differentiates between normal and severe grief. Normal grief is uncomplicated and does not require intervention to heal. Severe grief lingers on and has adverse effects on the grieving person. The latter condition requires intervention.

Worden goes on to explain the manifestations of both. Disbelief, confusion, preoccupation, a sense of presence and hallucinations are some of the effects of persistent grief which could trigger feelings that can lead to depression and anxiety, according to Worden. These facts are necessary as sources of information and important for forming a significant understanding.

Peter L. Steinke

This brings us to another resource, *How the Church Family Works: Understanding Congregations as Emotional Systems*, written by Peter L. Steinke. In this book, Steinke shows how what happens to us outside the church manifests itself in our fellowships. Our emotions have effects on each other and how we deal with them, has impact on the wellness or the un-wellness of the congregation.

A conclusion can be made from this argument that the nature of our care to the grieving members of the church will determine how our congregations as "emotional systems" will function. The reasoning is that if one is sick, hurting or grieving, we are all grieving. Paul, the apostle argues and rightly so that the body is a unit and if one part is paining, the whole body is paining (1Cor 12: 12ff). None of our members are dispensable or spared when it comes down to such matters as bereavement.

The truth is that we constantly influence each other, that we either hurt or help each other.[14] Steinke gives useful guidelines on how congregations can design ways of dealing with stress and anxiety and how spiritually and emotionally healthy leaders can influence the emotional systems of the congregation. Much relevance can be drawn between Steinke's material and the possible effects of those who are grieving in a congregation and what adverse effects they transfer to the rest of the members of the fellowship.

Howard Clinebell

Howard Clinebell offers a very sound and foundational basis for pastoral care and counseling. He explains the biblical roots of the six dimensions of wholeness namely: "relational wholeness, ecological wholeness, liberation, spiritual

---

[14] Peter Steinke, *How Your Church Family Works: Understanding Congregations as Emotional Systems* (The Hemdon, VA: Alban Institute, 2006), 40.

wholeness, physical wholeness and mental wholeness."[15] These "wholenesses" are dependent on when the unlikely happens and more so during times of loss.

Clinebell also talks about wholeness as depicted in the New Testament and especially in the phrase, "the kingdom of God". "This is an age of caring community, of justice and social transformation based on a new wholeness making relationship with God".[16] The church is the place where people come for healing. It is the body of Christ the Healer and thus depends on and looks unto him for healing.

Grief needs healing; mourning needs someone to wipe away the tears. The suffering person's hand needs someone to hold. The shoulder needs a pat. The body needs someone to lean on to. Someone needs to provide a rug on which to stand. Someone needs to provide a rail on which to hold. Christ wants the church to perform these tasks. Clinebell dedicates a whole chapter on bereavement care and counseling (chapter 9, pp. 218-242). He states the seriousness of bereavement by quoting psychiatrist Erich Lindemann, a pioneer in grief research:

> Studies show that many people become sick following the death of a loved one. A great many more hospital patients have had a recent bereavement than people in the general population. And in psychiatric hospitals, about six times as many are recently bereaved than in the general population...Furthermore, in a great many conditions, both physical and

---

[15] See Howrd Clinsbell. *The Basics of Pastoral care and counseling: Resources for the Ministry of Healing and Growth* (Nashville, TN: Abingdon Press 1994) pp.52-55 in his description of the six dimensions of wholeness.

[16] Ibid.,61.

psychological, the mechanics of grieving play a significant role.[17]

Clinebell also gives outlines on strategies that can be followed in "setting up and leading a grief healing group"[18] His suggestions were useful in meeting the final goal of this book. Emphasizing group care and counseling, Clinebell quotes from Matthew 18:20 (NIV): "For where two or three are gathered in my name, there am I in the midst of them". He also refers to Col. 2:2 to convey the importance of God's people coming together and encouraging each other in love. The significance of support groups cannot be stated in a better way than Clinebell has put it:

> Group caring and counseling methods constitute the single most useful resource for broadening and deepening a church's ministry of healing and growth. Group approaches applied to a wide spectrum of crises and issues in living can allow a church to become an increasing force for preventing personality problems by stimulating growth toward wholeness. Exciting developments are occurring in the use of small groups in some congregations. But most churches have only scratched the surface of the rich possibilities for small group ministries. [19]

The book, *How to Recover from Grief*,[20] by Richard L Detrich and Nicola J Steele is another valuable source. This

---

[17] Ibid., 4.
[18] Clinebell, 227-230.
[19] Ibid., 349
[20] Richard L. Detrich, *How to Recover from Grief*, Revised Edition (Valley Forge, PA: Judson Press, 1996

book serves as both a source of information as well as a workbook. It covers most of what we need to know about grief. It goes over all the phases of grief: shock, anger, guilt, bargaining, reconciliation, acceptance and also touches on a very important area, growing through grief. Both authors talk about how to mourn, giving suggestions such as: keeping a journal, make a history, make a memorial, seeking a closure amongst several others.

They also suggest ways in which to help another through grief and how to start a grief recovery group. These suggestions were helpful to this project as they gave direction to further develop the ultimate goal, of forming groups to reach and help others.

Larry Kent Graham in his book, *Care of Persons, Care of Worlds: A Psycho-Systems Approach to Pastoral Care and Counseling*[21] also offers very good insights. The writer moves from the premise: what affects one, has a ripple effect on one's associations and relations including the environment. This environment as far as our venture is concerned is the community of faith, referred to as the Church.

Graham sees symptoms as signs that something is not right. Depression can be a symptom of rage and grief can be a symptom of love or deep attachment. He sees symptom formation as occurring in three phases: the onset phase when a dissonance occurs (loss of a loved one) and breeds into anxiety and pain; the escalation phase when the symptom manifests itself in greater pain and more destabilization, and finally, the resolution phase when equilibrium is restored, and a sense of normalcy returns.

During the loss of a loved one, this can be no better

---

[21] Larry Kent Graham, *Care of Persons, Care of Worlds: A Psycho systems Approach to Pastoral Care and Counseling* (Nashville, TN: Abingdon Press, 1992).

applied. If the bereaved does not have a chance to share in the bidding of farewell to the deceased, the matter can be further exacerbated if left unattended. Graham shows how pastoral care is a mandate given to the pastor from God and offers ways in which the pastor can bring health to the grieving party.[22]

Betty Carter in her book co-authored with Monica McGoldrick, *The Expanded Family Life Cycle*,[23] (chapters 11 and 12), gives some very useful information about death and how it interferes adversely with the family life cycle. The latter chapter discusses ways in which rituals can be used in easing and healing the grief. In the chapters, she elevates, and rightly so, the place of rituals in healing and out of this, the therapy/support group has come out with concrete rituals that can be performed to heal the bereaved as well as the congregation. In concluding chapter 12 of her book, Carter states:

> Therapy needs conversations about meaningful rituals. Creative and sensitive crafted rituals both borrow richly from normative life cycle rituals and are simultaneously new. They facilitate necessary transitions and the expansion of relationship possibilities.[24]

Rituals are what remain when everything else is forgotten. Their importance cannot be over-emphasized. This group

---

[22] See Graham pp. 93-111 where he explains at length signs of grief and how a pastor can help those in it.

[23] Betty Carter and Monica McGoldrick Eds., *The Expanded family Life Cycle:*
Individual, Family, and Social Perspectives, Third Edition (Boston: Allyn and Bacon, 1999).

[24] Betty, 213

referred to in this book came up and performed some rituals to help themselves in the transition from disease to relief.

Howard Stone in *Strategies of Brief Pastoral Counseling*[25] gives an overview of the seven-dimension paradigm in caregiving and counseling as well as in all aspects of ministry which he says cultivates healing and nurturing the wholeness of those who receive care.

The dimensions, similar to Clinebell's, address the spirit (to "deepen roots into God's marvelous love" [Ephesians 3:17, NIV]), the mind, the body, love (heart), work and play and the world in which healed persons can help to heal the world. Stone invites his readers (pastors) to encourage sharing, inviting and being open to change and being involved in God Talk: listening for and talking about faith. Stone's models were very appropriate for our target group who mourn without the body "with outstretched arms groping for support." Through the model:

> Congregational ministers offering brief pastoral counseling collaborate with parishioners' understanding of their problems and goals for the future, invite change, and open space for new meanings and more faithful action. The not-knowing therapeutic approach toward parishioners' expertise in their own experience and goals, an essential element of brief pastoral counseling is balanced with appropriate knowing and claiming faith perspectives.
>
> As collaborators, pastoral caregivers shape the content and direction of pastoral encounters

[25] Howard W. Stone, *Strategies for Brief Pastoral Counseling* (Minneapolis: Fortress Press 2001).

with brief references to faith, biblical images, questions, and comments concerning parishioners' sense of who God is and how God is acting in relation to the problem they face. In this way, congregational ministers doing brief pastoral counseling participate in what God is calling forth within their troubled parishioners' lives. They anticipate the new creation as, together, they speak of it, look for it, and respond in faith. A new story begins.[26]

Stone's model summarizes the three components of our project as an act of ministry in which God, the church and the pastor are involved. The latter two are important collaborators of the work God is doing in the world and particularly to and with those who are suffering. Their role is to represent and present God to them.

John S Mbiti commits a whole chapter to "death and the hereafter". According to Mbiti in his book, *African Religions and Philosophy*,[27] states that, the majority of African people treat their dead with a lot of respect. This is because "a person dies and yet he/she continues to live; he/she is living-dead, and no other term can describe the dead person better."[28]

There is a very close mystical affinity African peoples have toward their departed. The world of the living (the *Sasa*-present) is not dichotomized from the world of the departed. These facts make it imperative for an African to be as close as possible to the departed especially before s/he finally disappears physically from sight on the day of the burial ceremony. Being there physically on such an occasion creates another sort of relationship:

---

[26] Ibid., 42.
[27] John S. Mbiti, *African Religions and Philosophy*, 1979.
[28] Mbiti, 161.

"I know you are gone, but you are still here." If one fails to attend the burial ceremony, s/he may never develop this special relationship. Mbiti's book coupled with Jomo Kenyatta's, *Facing Mount Kenya*, were other sources for material about what goes on after the funerals and the rituals that take place.

Both these books informed the author about some practices that were there in the pre-colonial period and how they were phased out or watered down to skeletons by the effect of Christianity. It is a challenge to resurrect some of those practices and use them to help heal mourners in our present times.

James W. Moore has written several devotionals. I have read several of his books. He is quite a good author. One that is particularly relevant to our venture is the one he has written about stress. Moore poses this question to the reader: *Is There Life after Stress?*[29] That too is the title of his book. The answer is obviously "yes," for many but when one is in stress, one must answer for her/himself Moore's opening paragraph goes:

> There's no question about it! We live in a stressful world, a turbulent world, in which we must learn to cope with the stresses of this life, or else we will be pulled apart at the seams. No one is immune. Stress is no respecter of persons. It touches the life of every person in one way or another.[30]

Moore's style in sermonizing on the various aspects of grief has many helpful hints on how to handle our support

---

[29] James W. Moore, *Is There Life After Stress?* (Nashville, TN: Dimensions for Living, 1992).
[30] Ibid.,9.

groups. He also has interesting stories and bible verses to share. These are but just a few of the many resources out there. More of them appear in the Bibliography.

I encourage the reader to explore more because every day there is a handy book, or a periodical article being released touching on pastoral caring to those undergoing tough or difficult situations. For the purposes of this book, let the above suffice for now.

6

Culture and Christianity Clash

Missionary Work

At the close of the 19th Century, Christian missionaries had begun entering the heartland of Kenya which was then a British colony. Most of the missionary activity took place in the central region of Kenya, the land of the Kikuyu (*Gikuyu* is the local name) tribe. In the early 20th century, almost every location had a mission station built up on a hill, towering above everything else.

It looked as if power and authority came from the hill and streamed down to the areas around it. It was like a recreation of the hill of Zion. From the hill flowed change.

From the hill emanated ideas and new and unfamiliar perspectives that changed the landscape of the whole region. The long tentacles from the hill entangled and almost strangled the life of the slopes, and unfortunately, they were unavoidable.

At the close of the 19th Century, Christian missionaries had begun entering the heartland of Kenya which was then a British colony. Most of the missionary activity took place in the central region of Kenya, the land of the Kikuyu (Gikuyu is the local name) tribe. In the early 20th century, almost every location had a mission station built up on a hill, towering above everything else.

The coming of Christianity brought the beginning of confusion and near chaos. Those who first converted to Christianity were thrown into a huge dilemma. Life was lived in communities but then came this new religion that required its converts to abandon and to move away from their communities emotionally and socially and become members of a new community called the church.

Moving out was like going into exile in one's own land. If that was not a big issue, the demand, for one to reject and to excise oneself from the traditions of his/her own people was. The demand for one to forsake his/her own tribe, relatives, and friends and not to get involved in their social gatherings, ceremonies, and celebrations of important community events of life was enough to jolt even the staunchest of the converts.

However, it happened and the tension and confusion and divisions it caused were enough to rip the tribe into two estranged factions. The most tension was felt as folk tried to determine what was tradition and what was Christian. Tension reigned everywhere especially in families that had a few converts and the rest being pagans (nonbelievers or *washenzi*), a new vocabulary hitherto unknown in the tribe. It was a derogatory term used to describe those who did not embrace the new faith and the new way of life; those outside the church.

These words from the book, *History of the Church in Africa*, by Jonathan Hildebrandt paint for us a portrait of the scenario:

> Turning to another aspect of Church history, in 1929 and 1930 there developed the

"circumcision crisis" in the central part of Kenya. The question was whether girls should be forced by the elders of the tribe to undergo circumcision.

The question had been raised long before 1929. 'From the earliest days missionaries of the church of Scotland Mission taught against female circumcision. The reasons given were medical, arising from the nature and after-effects of the operation. By 1912, this teaching had begun to have effect on the younger girls in mission boarding schools.

In June 1914, two girls expressed their wish to abandon the operation. However, both missionaries and the leaders of the small, baptized community felt that the time had not yet come for the outright rejection of the rite in public. So, it was agreed by the girls, their parents and the circumcisers that the operation should be performed in Kikuyu hospital by the usual circumcisers and with Christian sponsors.

The same procedure was adopted in 1915, but on this occasion one of the girls lost her nerve and underwent the operation with great reluctance. She was extensively cut and so the experiment was not repeated. A similar experiment was made in Tumutumu, and in 1915, three girls were operated on by tribal circumcisers.

Dr. Phillip who witnessed the operation found it so brutal that he refused to sanction its being repeated and therefore subsequently opposed the custom by every means in his power. This led to reviews of policy by the churches, and in March 1916, the church committees at Kikuyu and Tumutumu recommended circumcision of baptized girls of Christian parents, or girls in mission schools, be made a matter of church discipline. It would seem that at the Gospel Mission station at Kambui, the A.I.M. station at Kijabe and the C.M.S. station at Kabete, the teaching proceeded along the same line'.

From 1916 until 1929 the churches continued to teach against female circumcision. In March 1929, the members of several denominations in Central Province met at Tumutumu to discuss the problem. It was agreed that the rite was evil and should no longer be practiced by Christians.

Then in June 1929, a girl at Kambui School was kidnapped on a public road and circumcised by force. The matter was taken to court, but the magistrate ruled against the Christians, which in effect said that the elders of the tribe could kidnap any girl they wanted to in future and have her circumcised.[31]

The controversy over female circumcision came with some resistance. Those who were against it, claiming it was part

---

[31] Jonathan Hildebrandt. *History of the Church in Africa* (Achimota, Ghana: African Christian Press, 1981), 231-232.

of their cultural and important rite of passage for girls into adulthood, and later marriage, formed a movement called the Kikuyu Central Association. Its main objective was to preserve the cultural practices, and norms of the Gikuyu people that they felt were being threatened by the *Nyaker*u (the white missionaries).

The Kikuyu Central Association (KCA was pro-circumcision and stood strongly in its defense. This was counter to the stand of the members of the church who argued vehemently against the rite. The outcome was that the whole of the Gikuyu country was upset by the divide caused by the contrary arguments. The controversy had immediate impediment to the progress and daily mission work that saw a significant drop in church and school attendance. The long-term effects were more impactful and far-reaching. The seed of separatism was sown. In that same year, 1929, the birth of the African Independent Churches was realized. The movement gained a lot of popularity and competed neck to neck with the foreign mission churches while maintaining the rite of female circumcision.

All the towns mentioned above are in Central Kenya and were and still are important and historic mission stations to this day. The A.I.M. is an acronym for African Inland Mission and C.M.S. stands for the Church Missionary Society. The situation was serious, no doubts about it. This serious division and confusion were spread to and affected all other spheres of life across the board.

It was not made any better by the rise and upsurge of the East African Revival Movement that happened at around the same time. This created a clear dichotomy between what was "Christian" and what was traditional. One was either Christian (saved) or traditional (pagan) but never both. If anyone crisscrossed the lines, s/he was thrown out, or alternatively had to denounce the other side publicly. During community ceremonies and celebrations, the distinction was very clear. It could be better seen, felt and experienced. Christians kept to themselves and so did the rest of the community.

Memorable Epoch

1929 marked a new era in the life of the Kikuyu people. The ounce of weight that broke the camel's back was added to an already overloaded animal. The big issue at stake was female circumcision. The matter was so serious that the community, families and even friends were ripped apart. Those in the church were forced to make a choice by forces beyond their control, whether to follow traditions and so observe the rite or to denounce it and remain loyal 'Christians'.

Those who chose the latter were to sign their name (kirore) in a book to clearly declare their stand. In some places, a line was drawn on the ground and one had to step or jump over it to show what side s/he belonged. Those who stepped over denounced their ties with the traditions and chose the new way, the way of those who had seen the light. This way of light came with its problems, too. It was hard for those who opted to adopt Christianity to tell that which was "Christian-culture or that which was European culture". Christianity in those days was inseparable from European culture, better known as western culture.

The two were synonymous. In fact, there was more western culture in Christianity than were Christian teachings and beliefs. During this time very few could read or write and so learned by hearing and observing what the "white man did and how he lived." This was taken as being representative of what Christianity was. The white people's culture became synonymous with the new religion. If one dressed, ate, drunk, slept or wore, associated with and spoke a word or two of the new tongue, the better s/he was as a Christian.

Let's go back a little to the circumcision tussle in the middle of the first half of the 20th century. Tension was pretty high. Churches split. The birth of independent churches has its nemesis or origin here. The independent churches wanted to create 'African Christians' and so kept the traditions and elements of the new faith. Those who chose to abandon the traditions became so anti-tradition that their theology became 'salvation from the devious/ evil/unholy/pagan/satanic/tribal practices'.

Everything foreign (English) was seen as the norm and therefore Christianity became western culture: style, manner of eating, dressing, living, behavior, talking and all what is western. The more one adopted and copied European culture, the better Christian s/he was seen to be.

In the Presbyterian Church of East Africa, the demarcation was distinct, very clearly defined. This was a Scottish Mission and adopted most of the Scottish culture especially in its religious practices. It is still the practice in most congregations today that if one were to take the pulpit s/he must be appropriately dressed in accordance with the practices of the church.

To cite but one example, a male preacher must be in tie, jacket, and appropriate shoes. A lady preacher should wear a headscarf and a sweater and a long dress. If the preacher deviates much from these norms, the elders are more likely to deny him/her the pulpit or allow him/ her to preach after some admonishment in the vestry and sometimes followed by an apology before the congregation.

European clothing became the Christian's clothing and soon the majority of the people followed suit. Christians started living the European way, ate the European way, smoked the European way, slept the European way. Huge changes were taking place and rather drastically. I remember wearing jeans or worse a bell-bottom, short skirts or a tight dress was seen as satanic. The way one dressed was seen as a reflection of how one believed.

Christianity Wins

Eventually, over decades, western culture took precedence in many areas. Western culture and lifestyle were equated with civilization and development and success. The churches were the vehicles that helped its entrenchment into the communities. Churches ran schools, health centers and other important centers that offered services to the people. Over time, the traditional started to thaw and western culture disguised as Christianity made inroads into the community life.

There was not much choice left. It was the case of "join them if you cannot beat them." Resistance was fierce and intense at the very beginning but decreased as colonialism and imperialist power became more embedded and spread its strong roots into all areas of central Kenya for better or for worse. Things were never the same again and never have been.

Change Has Come

The surge of western culture and its widespread influence in the central parts of Kenya had overcome all else. The second and third generations of Christians lost much of what was traditional and adopted what was western. Marriages, education, construction of homes, celebrations of funerals and burials, took a different approach. Coupled with urbanization that was taking place at the same time, life seemed to be changing very fast and with troubling, at times turbulent, twists and turns.

The mobility of people largely spiked. It was triggered by the changing economic landscape that brought with it a different perspective of life. The current was so strong to counteract, and people had no choice left other than to flow with it.

While it was the practice to mourn openly and loudly and express one's grief to all, this practice suffered a death knell especially with the influx of the aforementioned East African Revival. This revival was the antithesis of anything Kikuyu (tribal/customary). Mourning, crying, tearing, grieving or any expressions of hurt or pain or sorrow were seen as anti-Christian and signs of defeat, weakness, and lack of faith.

Such were pagan practices, and all saved Christians were discouraged from displaying them. Such were behaviors and practices of people without hope. Christians had hope of resurrection and so should not mourn because it was, just for a while and then they would meet with the departed brother/sister in heaven. Mourning was a sign of disbelief. After all, Christ mourned for us and took away our grief. We (Christians) should be brave and bold for we have triumphed over death.

Instead of mourning, we should rejoice and give thanks and sing praise songs because the deceased has gone to live with the Lord. This was their new doctrine and understanding of death. Thessalonians 4: 13-18 became a popular passage and the key line most cited was verse 13, "we do not grieve like the rest of men."

During funerals, the bereaved were expected to give testimonies of "courage" and "immovability" and "victory." They were to sing and praise, exuding joy and no signs of worry or grief. If such signs were present, such moaners would be deemed as succumbing to despair and defeat and even be counted as having fallen from grace. They would be seen as "grieving like the rest of men, who have no hope."

It might seem monotonous or repetitious to keep mentioning 1929 but because that year marked the turning point of the history of the Kikuyu community, it serves a purpose to keep referring to it for the sake of understanding our argument here. The period after the big division of 1929 (the issue of female circumcision was the key problem) caused a great rift between communities and families.

Life was divided between whether one chose to live a traditional way or whether one opted for the western way (Christian style). Brother was separated from brother, sister from sister, even a son/daughter from a parent. It was not unusual for a parent to choose not to attend the wedding of a son/daughter because s/he did not belong to the same camp, sect or brand of faith.

In extreme cases, even funerals of close relatives were boycotted by certain members of the same family or clan because they belonged to the wrong camp. This practice has not died away completely especially within the conservatives from both wings. Members of the East African Revival were notorious here. They did not want anything to do with any community activities outside their camp. Some remnants or pockets of this practice still exist in some areas.

Difficult to Keep Balance

It is difficult to minister in such an atmosphere. It is not easy to keep the balance between the tensions without the danger of being seen as leaning too much to one side. There is some general consensus within religious circles that a pastor is called to minister, first to her/his church and second to the community at large. Both roles require equal treatment and call for a delicate balance if one is to really be seen as "becoming all things to all men":

19Though I am free and belong to no man, I make myself a slave to everyone, to win as many as possible. 20To the Jews I became like a Jew, to win the Jews. To those under the law (though myself I am not under the law), so as to win those under the law. 21To those not having the law I became like one not having the law (though I am not free from God's law but under Christ's law), so as to win those not having the law. 22To the weak I became weak, to win the weak. I have become all things to all men so that by all possible means I might save some. 23I do all this for the sake of the gospel; that I may share in its blessings. (1 Cor. 9:19-23) (NEB).

The local pastor has for a long while been seen as an important person within his/her own community. It is everyone's perception that s/he is there for all. Sometimes the pastor overreaches his/her assumed boundaries especially as perceived by his/her church leaders and may be accused of having fallen from grace if he "cohabitates" with the community outside the church to a degree that makes the leadership feel uncomfortable if not insecure. They may accuse the pastor of being too compromised. The pastor no doubt has a huge responsibility that is coupled with many risks sometimes emanating from very unlikely sources. Most pastors particularly those from mainstream churches serve beyond their denominational boundaries and "become pastors of the people."

Ministering in such an atmosphere becomes a big challenge. Although as argued above a good minister has to take care of the flock within as well as reach out to those who do not belong, striking a balance between these two ministries to the satisfaction of all concerned is a delicate matter. The risk of being misunderstood or misconceived is enormous.

The point that I am driving at is that the methods of giving pastoral care vary from place to place and largely depend on the composition of the constituency and the degree to which the influence of Christianity has reached in any particular area. By an accident of history and geography, I happen to belong to an area and to a denomination (Presbyterian) where the two forces were distinct and deeply felt.

On the one hand, mourning in a traditional way was a community task or responsibility. The mourners were encouraged to voice and express their grief in every manner and volume possible. The family, the clan, the community stood with them during the funeral and long after the burial was over. It went on for close to a month if not more until the bereaved were able to function on their own. On the other hand, here was the "Church," the "New way." The usual time before the burial was cut short.

Church members were discouraged from expressing any sad feelings or grief. Grieving was therefore turned into a private matter. Instead of grief being externalized, it became internalized. Instead of close relatives and the community helping and standing with the bereaved, the community of faith that at times lived miles apart and only assembled for worship vainly filled the gap.

Individuals who were bereaved suffered alone, mourned alone; grieved in seclusion. They hid their feelings in order not to be called 'ye of little faith.' This practice led to many of them developing serious health conditions. No one was wiser. It was a transition to nowhere, because no one had a hold or control over what was happening. There was no particular way to do things, let alone to mourn. But then, who suffered most other than the common Christian who was torn between two conflicting worlds?

Mixed Model

That was one side of the coin. The ministers of the mainstream denominations who chose to denounce everything traditional (without which acceptance into church ministerial office would be a pipe dream) were trained in theological colleges at home and abroad, that were largely western. The same training exposed them to western methods of doing and giving pastoral care, a method which is largely therapeutic. There is no better way of describing this model than Emmanuel Lartey has in his book, In Living Color: *An Intercultural Approach to Pastoral Care and Counseling:*

> Under this model, the task of the pastoral caregiver is to remove, or correct, what is wrong and in some way or by some means to return the sufferer to functioning order. Essentially the caregiver is there to make us better. The helper has a Messianic function. He or she heals, helps or saves us or enables us to be healed, helped or saved. An assumption of this model is that it is possible to achieve the goals it seeks, so that by divine assistance, divine grace, or else some form of divine intervention, things can be made better. Where the divine is not invoked it is assumed that there are naturally occurring substances, or ways of behavior or thought, which are invested with the power to correct the malfunction.

The caregiver's task is to discover and to administer or recommend these to patients or clients. The strength of this model lies in the fact that it offers a clear and understandable 'problems' to which there is a 'solution.' It is premised upon first, diagnosing or recognizing, what is wrong and then investing in a solution. Without an acknowledgement of a problem, there is no solution to be sought.[32]

There are scanty literary materials about how the process of death, mourning and grieving took place. In my research, I found material about death and the rituals that followed before and shortly after disposing of the body, but never came across material narrating how the mourning and grieving was handled, especially as pertains to the Kikuyu group of peoples. While Mbiti, *African Religions and Philosophy* is too general, Kenyatta's, *Facing Mount Kenya*, unfortunately left this portion out.

However, as mentioned earlier in several places in this book, one of the most conspicuous expressions of grief in many African peoples is that it was generally expressed and openly done. Some tribes are known to even have professional mourners to help those grieving. But times and circumstances have changed, Death has not, and still remains what it is, death. In one way or another, the community helped the grieving on their journey toward healing.

It is not easy to practice what Mbiti or Kenyatta have written but several facts can be lifted. First the grieving process takes a long time. Several things need to be done to facilitate the healing process. There is need for some

---

[32] Emmanuel Y. Lartey, *In Living Color: An Intercultural Approach to Pastoral Care and Counseling, Second Edition* (London: Athenaeum Press, 2003), 55-56.

appropriate rituals to be performed before the day of the funeral. There is also a need to stand with the bereaved for some time. The length of time will depend on how fast they recover. Above all there is dire need to encourage them to openly express their grief especially in its initial stages.

For the purpose for which this book was written and given the circumstances surrounding it and the factors and people involved, it was unsuitable to use one model as opposed to another. The best way was to use the model or a combination of models that brought out the best possible results. Scooping a bit from the traditional and adding it to the western therapeutic model thus forming a mix of both, at times distinct, at other times indistinguishable, would be the best route to take.

All that was available to us and was helpful and worked towards the best achievements of the functions of Pastoral care: healing, sustaining, guiding, reconciling, nurturing, liberating, and empowering, was made use of. Peter Van Lierop, *Pastoral Counseling: A Comprehensive Text for Pastors, Counselors and Teachers*, puts it in a better way and helps explain my thoughts in fewer words:

> The pastor also assists the bereaved person face the reality of his situation and to think through the deeper meanings of his new responsibilities, new relationships and new problems of adjustments. The pastor can be like a sounding board against which the mourner can work out his new thoughts and feelings. The mourner needs to express his feelings of sorrow and sense of loss and to verbalize his feelings of guilt.

Relationships to the church can be encouraged by the pastor for this will help in dealing with guilt and mourning. The pastor can help replace despair with hope, fearfulness with faith and guilt with forgiveness. It is also very essential to help the mourner find a substitute for the loss he has sustained. The grieving person can be assisted and inspired to live and work creatively and meaningfully, thereby finding a fulfilling life that is really worthwhile and satisfying.[33]

Life is dynamic. Life is never static. There is always something going on. Changes are inevitable and will always come and will continue to come as long as life endures, and time unfolds. Changes call for adjustments on our part. Sometimes adjustments are painful, but all the same necessary. Pastoral caregiving has to change with time.

Sometimes it calls for combinations of methods especially if the recipient belongs to two or more worlds, the old and the new, the secular and the sacred, the familiar and the unfamiliar, the stable and the unpredictable. A combination of traditional and the western therapeutic methods of care for someone who has one foot in America and the other in Africa was the right path to take.

I received a text the other day from a young man of 26 years that at first horrified me. The young man told me, "I feel low, lost, heartbroken, and stressed out. At times I feel like I'd want to harm myself. Please call me. I need someone to talk to." I called the young person immediately and he picked up the phone. He started crying, the kind of cry that comes

---

[33] Peter van Lierop, *Pastoral Counseling: A Comprehensive Text for Pastors, Counselors, Teachers* (Nairobi: The Christian Churches Educational Association, 1992), 102.

from deep down a sorrowful heart, the cry that touches the very depths of one's empathetic nerve.

I gave him time to cry and when he was able to say a word, he said sadly, "I have no family here. I had one friend who was with me for five years but now she has left me. I feel alone. I feel afraid. I am in despair. I have no one to turn to. Both my parents died in the last four years. I never traveled home to bury them. I have no one to comfort or encourage me.

The only one who can understand me is gone and wants nothing to do with me." He started to cry again. I said, though rather unconvincingly, "I am here for you." After a lull, he said, "You are my family. You are the only person I can openly say this to. If I am doing this project today, I would have at least included one or two young people who came to the United States to study, overstayed their visas and got held up here.

They are unfortunately not spared losses through death of their loved ones. They are there my dear pastors, in our cities, in our neighborhoods, in our churches, in our communities. I urge you to look out for them and be there for them. They need your support. I am hopeful this tool will assist you towards that end.

A Description of the Project

To carry out the project in a systematic and coherent manner, planning was of the essence. The group needed to be built, meetings had to be initiated and a methodology had to be defined. The group should know who they are, why they are and where they are going and how to get there. Without this prior planning and understanding, the results might not have been as intended or realized.

The first step taken was to develop a questionnaire and identify the responders amongst those who have lost their loved ones. The criterion we used was to choose those who had lost immediate family member(s) and those who had lost multiple members. In all, a group of eight was ideal (though dealing with smaller groups would be better). The next thing was to meet with the selected group individually and explain to them the process, give each of them the questionnaire and allow them two weeks to respond and mail it back.

The next step was to meet with the group and schedule the number of sessions we were to have and when. By the time of writing this chapter the group had moved from that stage and we had already agreed to meet at least four times for 2 hours each time.

During each session, each of the group members was to have ten minutes to contribute and share one's feelings following the questionnaire. The group was to spend the rest of the time for responses.

The group also agreed that more time would be added if the need arose. Even if timing was an important discipline to exercise, the course we were undertaking would at times require us to go beyond the scheduled time. The group believed that since grieving at times takes its natural course and defies the dictates of set times and schedules, flexibility on our part, was imperative. This happened in a couple of our meetings as the report below about our meetings will reveal.

Below is our a tentative schedule:

Session	Topic/Discussion	Remarks
One	How did you receive the sad news? Respond to questions 1-4	How would you have liked to receive the news?
Two	How did you share the news? What help and support did you get? Respond to questions; 5-9	Evaluation of the support.
Three	How did you grieve? What is your stage of grief? Respond to questions 10-15	How can we help each other to overcome grief?
Four	How can we help others (church members) facing similar situations? Respond to questions 16-17	Work out a strategy of helping others.

Five	How was the process helpful for you?	Each to respond in writing and share with the group. Each to give a rating on a scale of 1-10 with 10 being the highest.

The group also suggested ways of moving forward in terms of helping others. The final session (session five) was to be particularly geared toward this goal. The measure of success for the project would be partly dependent on the group's enthusiasm and participation in the process as well as their response to the evaluation questions:

1. Was the process important for you?
2. If it was valuable, why and how?
3. How do you feel now?
4. Has anything changed from the time you started this process until now?
5. How would you rate the process on a scale of 1-10, ten being the highest?

Four key areas would be used to determine the success of this project. The Overall effect will be felt if not seen in how the members live out their lives in the future and how they get involved or react when the next victim of "mourning without the body' appears on the scene. However, these four areas will be important in measuring the success of the project at the end of the process.

1. The development of a useful tool (documented) to help others in grief.
2. The competence of the 8 participants in using the tool.
3. The response and especially the rating of the participants to the questions above.

4. Whether the participants will identify their grief and freely express it during and after the process.

All the above constitute the desired results and direction. However, even the best thought-out and well-organized plans, take a different direction, slightly off the intended course. At times the process might not be all completed within the set time. But all said and done, the intended ways and means are as laid out above.

Initiating the Process

The process began on the premise that these people were in need of help (those grieving without the body). The pastor (Rev. Joseph Kimatu) assisted by a few church leaders identified eight victims with this kind of grief. Our meeting took place on Thursday, Oct. 8, 2009. The eight comprised the group that had lost one or two persons back in Kenya and did not have an opportunity to go and attend their funerals. Only those who had suffered this kind of loss in the past three years were considered.

The first two selected had lost a parent or both parents in the year 2007. The second set of four lost either a spouse/sibling or parent in 2008 and the last pair lost theirs in the current year, 2009. We had noted a slight change in the way they participated and socialized within the church and community.

It was clear to those assisting the pastor that since their losses, they had tended to slow down in their church attendance and participation. They looked lonely and seemed aloof and disinterested. The church leaders and the pastor prayed for the project and those eight asking that God would grant that they willingly participate in the project and that they would find healing in the process.

The pastor approached the eight and invited them to the first meeting. All eight of them turned up for our first session on Thursday Nov. 5, 2009, at 4:00 pm. After the usual introductions and casual acquaintance stuff, the pastor called the group to order. After devotion and prayer, the minister explained the purpose of the meeting as:

a) Meeting for several sessions and work through our grief. We all had one common denominator. We have lost our loved ones and never saw them buried.
b) To schedule our sessions accordingly, our availability being the major factor.
c) At the end of the process, to come out with a plan on how we can be of help to others suffering the same fate. If we could develop such a document, the ministry of the project would continue.

In this session we all agreed to be faithful to the process. We also agreed to respond to the questionnaire provided and bring our answers to our first and subsequent sessions. This questionnaire is in Appendix 1 as well:

1. How did you receive the news?
2. Had you any warnings something "bad" was going to happen prior to the death(s)?
3. Describe briefly what the warnings were if your answer to question 2 is yes.
4. What was your first reaction?
5. With whom did you share the news?
6. Who mourned with you?
7. Was the community/family/church support helpful to you?

8. How did it help you?
9. Was there anything negative about this support?
10. How did you feel about not viewing or being present with the family for the funeral and burial?
11. Have you overcome your grief?
12. If yes, how long did it take to overcome it?
13. If not, how strong is it?
14. What did you find most helpful in overcoming the grief?
15. What did you find least helpful?
16. What can you say to someone in similar circumstances?
17. How can the church/community help in supporting those in grief?

Before engaging on the process, as is noted earlier in this book, I had made a futile attempt in approaching a number of pastors requesting them to fill out a questionnaire for me (Appendix 3). I call it futile because almost all shied away from the exercise, but I am thankful to God that one of them, a Brazilian immigrant was happy and willing to hearken to my cry.

The pastor had a Brazilian community church, and he was generous enough to share with us what transpired when death abroad invaded their shores. I think it is important to include his responses here for comparison and appreciation of the fact that some effort is done to "support the groping hand" although there seems like there is no apparent set structure for doing so. This is how he responded in his own words to the questionnaire, I sent. (See the unedited copy in Appendix 4):

Q. What is the initial response of the bereaved? What emotions are apparent?

A. The initial response is a deep feeling of a big loss, being away when good celebrations are happening back in their countries. This is not something that an immigrant can handle more easily; it's difficult to handle the feelings of the loss of a loved one. People desire to be close to their relatives for mutual support because being away increases the feeling of loss.

Those who have been away from their countries for many years, have a feeling of guilt for not being able to give emotional support to their relatives in their time of suffering. They feel guilty for not being able to give the last hug or last kiss to the people who passed away.

Q. As a pastor what is your initial response/intervention and what do you initiate?

A. This depends on who I'm going to give support. People react differently to this kind of situation. But, in general, I allow then to put away their feelings and, as they are doing that, I try to let them bring to their mind the good memories that will be forever in their hearts as it was at the heart of the deceased person.

Q. How does the church respond?

A. I was a pastor of a church of immigrants here in the USA for 10 years. The church response was firstly through providing companionship; practicing what the bible teaches us to do, weeping with those who weep. In some cases, it's possible that the church helps, families back in their country by providing some financial support for the funeral. This could happen also if the deceased person lived here. But I believe that companionship is the best way to give support to the bereaved.

Q. How does the community respond?

A. When the community is called to support it does so in a very good way. Solidarity is strong in times of this kind of suffering. When it is needed, the church may do some kind of activity, like a special kind of fundraising. The support is not only from the church's members, but from the outsiders too, the Brazilian community within the city and even outside if the deceased's family is well known by many.

Q. Are there any set procedures in your church for long term care to families whose loved ones pass overseas?

A. No. We never had something like that.

Q. Are there any special rituals that the bereaved or the church does to console the family or the bereaved?

A. We used to do a special service in memory of the deceased. This could be at the bereaved family's home, but the church was the venue for most of the memorial services I conducted.

Q. For families who are not able to travel for funeral and burial of their loved one(s), is there any special care that you provide to them?

A. This kind of situation is very common. Usually, the family could not travel because of their immigration statuses. Besides the funeral service, as the pastor, I used to visit several times the bereaved family or person, other members of the church would also do the same. This is important to let those in loss not feel lonely.

Q. How does not being able to travel affect the bereaved as opposed to those who are able to travel?

A. I believe that the feeling of grief will last longer, because they were not able to do the ritual to give back to the "dust" what was dust.

Q. Does your church have a "Grief/Bereavement Support Group"? How helpful is it to those unable to travel?
A. No, I didn't have a special group. I believe that in situations like this a group is formed spontaneously.

Q. What workable advice would you give to the church for it to be helpful to those grieving and unable to travel to join their families for funeral/burial observances?
A. A special service in memoriam would be very helpful. Also, as in many cases their families back in their respective countries are poor, providing some financial support to their families would give those who are here and unable to travel the feeling that they are doing something, and they are useful.

Q. What else do you think is helpful to such a group?
My Comment: The Pastor did not respond to this question for reasons I do not know.

Q. What reasons cause the inability of those unable to travel?
A. Financial problems, time's inability and immigration statuses are the main reasons. For time's inability I mean that in some countries, the law orders that the deceased shall be buried in hours. So, there is no time available to travel and to arrive before the funeral.

The questionnaire for the pastors was intended to get a sense of what is done in such circumstances that I thought would be useful to the process. The following will now be an intentional way of a possible handling of such cases that can be used to help pastors and congregations in supporting their members when loss abroad knocks on their doors. This explains the way the group of eight and I went through.

First, I had to come up with a possible calendar of events. The meetings were scheduled for Thursdays at 4 pm on

November 19, December 3, and 17, 2009 and January 7 and 21, 2010. This tentative schedule for our meetings was presented to the group. They accepted it and promised to adhere to it. It causes no harm to repeat it here to refresh our memory.

Session	Topic/Discussion	Remarks
One	How did you receive the sad news? Respond to Questions 1-4	How would you have liked to receive the news?
Two	How did you share the news? What help and support did you get? Respond to Questions 5-9	Evaluation of the support.
Three	How did you grieve? What is your stage of grief? Respond to Questions 10-15	How can we help each other to overcome grief?
Four	How can we help others (church? members) facing similar situations? Respond to Questions 16-17	Work out a strategy of helping others.
Five	How was the process helpful for you?	Each to Respond in writing and share with the group. Each to give a rating on a scale of 1-10 with 10 being the highest.

The highlight of this first meeting was a ritual symbolizing our journey together and the source of our strength and hope. The pastor had brought a bowl, some sand, a cross and some broken small stones. He put sand in the bowl and planted the cross right in the middle.

He then asked each of the group members in turn to pick a small broken stone and to place it under the cross. When all the stones were placed including the pastor's, the pastor asked what the process meant for them. All said almost a unanimous thing: "We are all in this together, broken as these stones, but at the cross, Christ will be there with us and thus helping us."

We agreed to place this bowl on the table throughout the sessions. The whole process of the ritual was a very solemn moment and some weeping occurred unprovoked. After heaves and sighs of relief, a long moment of silence so surreal and so heavy that one could cut with a knife ensued.

It seemed sacred and no one dared interrupt it. As time ticked away, we found ourselves growing closer and spontaneously, as if groping for support we held hands, prayed together, and departed silently to meet after two weeks.

I was left wondering if we had started on a journey we couldn't finish. I also wondered why so many tears would flow this long after the event. It was as if the deaths occurred the day before. Everything seemed so fresh. As the group filed out, I felt lonely and yearned for company.

Where was this leading to?

Session 1

The next two weeks were like eternity to me. I also learned from telephone conversations with about five of the members that they too couldn't wait either. On November 19, 2009, everyone turned up before the scheduled time. Some were more than half an hour early. We were all eager to get started. We had 20 minutes of devotion led by one of the participants, and she read from 1 Peter 5:6-7: "Humble yourselves, therefore, under God's mighty hand, that he may lift you up in due time. Cast all your anxiety on him because he cares for you" (NIV).

She emphasized that the death of her mother and not being there to bury her was a very humbling experience and she has learned since then to cast all her worries, sorrow and grief, even anger and guilt to the Lord. She testified that God has been lifting her up and she is no longer where she started. All of those present resonated with her testimony and shared almost the same experience.

After prayer and exchanging the usual pleasantries, we turned to answering the four questions set for the day. All the responses to question # 1 were almost identical. Participants received calls from a third party, designated by their families back in Kenya, but living here in the United States. It was hard on them to receive the sad news and even harder to call home.

In response to question # 2, the majority said they had received signals (undefined premonitions) akin to what they call telepathy, that all was not well, and something was bound to happen, the nature of which one could not tell clearly. A few said their sixth sense had informed them that something was not right. In response to Question # 3, they said they felt uneasy, anxious, and spiritually disturbed.

Question # 4 drew a lot of emotional reactions.

The responses were slow, deep, and sometimes choking and strangling. "Crying" was the key word, but shouting, falling down, helplessness, hopelessness, the urge to commit suicide, screaming, shock, speechlessness was some of the other words used. It was a moment of sadness, tears, and silence and perhaps sobriety for all of us.

We held hands together, kept silence for two minutes and said the grace together in unison and ended on that note, but I could tell all of us were relieved for having talked, let out our emotions, and relived that experience in a verbal and expressive manner. Although in African cultures, grief is shared amongst relatives and neighbors and crying out sometimes loudly thus leaving the grieving persons relieved, in a foreign land, it does not work out that way always. I would think if one wailed loudly, his/her neighbors would call 911 and the wailer will most likely be mistaken as having some psyche issues and taken to hospital for mental assessment.

Most of the folk, not having relatives or close confidants, usually grieve alone in silence and in isolation. To make matters worse, there is no time to mourn due to the nature of the setup of the system in America. Immigrants usually, juggle their time between two or three jobs. If one is lucky, s/he gets three days off work to grieve. But before one knows it, s/he is back to work with their wounds of grief fresh, open, and bleeding and probably prone to infection by 'germs' from other pressures of life, so to speak.

The fact that one has been grieving and had a few days off work does not relieve one of one's duty to pay his/her bills and on time. The group suggested they would rather have preferred to receive the news from their pastors, but unfortunately the folk back in Kenya do not always have his/her contacts. Unfortunately, some immigrant pastors also work two or three jobs in order to make ends meet.

They do twice as much work as their flock and yet they are expected to do good work by their churches. It is no wonder that those who lose their loved ones do not get all the support they need. They grieve longer than normal and so all of us in the group agreed that this process was unique and very important to us

Session 2

Our third meeting started on a high note. This group was getting ever closer. The atmosphere was getting more relaxed, and the fellowship seemed healthier. We were all early arrivals and bonded together well before the start of the meeting that happened on time. One of the group members led us in prayer and another shared the word from Philippians 4: 4-7. The key theme was "surrendering to God in prayer and let go our worries and let God take care."

It was very uplifting, and I could see heads nod in agreement to the message. After the session was called to order, one of the members, Judy (not her real name) asked if it was to add two items to the business of the day. We all agreed with her. It was our meeting, and all ideas were welcome as we progressed.

Judy suggested we should be holding short reviews on our previous meeting(s) and that at the end of each session we should be having a meal together. We were all for the latter, but we decided to write our personal evaluations and do a report at the end of all our sessions. That would keep our process on track.

In response to question # 5, most respondents said they shared the news with the pastor and some friends. Only two said they talked about it with their workmates. They said the church community (Kenyan), a few local friends and some members of their families came to mourn with them. The church was the most prominent group. Whether the support given was helpful, we all answered in the affirmative, but a few said it was hurting because it reminded them that they were not able to get to their clan, family, and community at home.

To some, the community that gathered to mourn with them was pseudo- community. It was not real for them. They felt they were given too much attention by people who hitherto had little time for them. Some said they felt as if they were being invaded and intruded upon and at the wrong time. They thought these people did not understand what they were going through. However, they got some spiritual support and financial help that they so desperately needed in the short run.

Question # 9 seemed a little difficult to respond to. It seemed like no one wanted to tell the truth on this one since some of the group members went to mourn at each other's houses. However, after assuring them we were in a safe place, perhaps even a sacred space, they began talking, but not without some hesitation.

Some said that those who came to mourn with them seemed emotionally detached or faked their feelings. Some said the services held were too formal and at times the messages irrelevant. Some said that some of the mourners turned the meetings into social gatherings and diverted attention to each other rather than focusing on the bereaved person(s).

Others felt these mourners came to give money just because they thought their turn would come and would be recipients of the same treatment in some sort of reciprocation by others, kind of a quid pro quo. Asked whether having no mourners to mourn with would be a better alternative, the room responded with a resounding "NO" as an answer. All said and done, such support and presence had its important place. It was more beneficial than otherwise. The financial aspect was met. The emotional not as much if at all.

We held hands together, and one of us said a parting prayer. During the two weeks that followed, I received phone calls from all eight group members. They all applauded the process and were happy about our meetings. They had also started communicating and visiting with each other. The group was no doubt bonding and uniting in the process.

Session 3

The next meeting took place on December 17, 2009. Judy and two others brought some food for our dinner together. They had organized it outside our meeting. This was a good sign. After devotion led by Ngigi who read from Psalm 23, we settled down to our fourth meeting together and the third session of the project. His message was hinged on the verses that transliterated / paraphrased would read: "God walks with us even in the valley of the shadow of death. God is our shepherd all the time, in all situations and will provide what we need always" (Ps. 23: 4-6, NIV).

In this session, we were to respond to questions 10-15. Everyone expressed regret that they were not able to attend the funeral, neither to participate by being present. All said they have not overcome the grief. On a scale of 1-10 on what stage of grieving process one had gotten to with one being at the bottom, all of us fell below 6. About a half of the group said the reality of their loss had not set in.

They still thought their deceased relatives were still alive and that someday they were going to meet each other. Some said that sometimes when they communicated with their families back in Kenya, they included the deceased on the list of those to be given their greetings only to be reminded that they passed. Some said that they even mentioned their names in their prayers and asked God to grant them long lives. It sounded weird and insane, but that was the reality. That which we hear sinks more slowly than that which we witness and participate in.

Asked about how we could help each other to bring about the irreversible reality of our losses, it seemed like no one had an answer. However, our being together and speaking out about our losses and grieving openly had helped some. Some suggested that we should imagine what the deceased would have told us if s/he knew we would not attend her/his funeral. The responses were: "You should not bother so much. I know that you love me, and I love you too. I know your situation and I understand. Even if I do not see you during my funeral, I will understand. My love for you will not diminish an iota. Spiritually, I will be with you. Do not ever feel guilty about it. Your God is my God, and we are both in God's hands. Somehow, God will one day join us together."

Some felt that our healing process had begun in earnest since we started working together. They even proposed continuing with our meetings and inviting others even after the project was done. Together, we felt we were getting more understanding and were doing relatively better in coping with our grief. Our coming together was turning out to be a great and invaluable opportunity to recreate community. As it was turning out, the Eight of us were turning into a family.

It is only in a loving family, where one feels comfortable, at ease and to belong. It is within a family setup where one can really let tears roll. In the family environment, one can shout, express oneself emotionally in all ways possible. This is hard to do elsewhere. It is only in a family setting where one feels secure enough because one is taken the way s/he is and not for granted. The family allows space to let out, speak it out, cry it out, weep it out, and moan it out. All those combined acts were like therapy to our grieving hearts.

It is in a group like this that the language that gives hope can be spoken. When someone dies, the Kikuyu community usually say, "S/he is gone on a journey or a visit, s/he has closed their eyes, s/he has gone to sleep, s/he has put their lights off, or s/he has decided to keep silent." All these phrases have the notion that death is only a temporary condition and at some point, the departed will re-emerge, return, or come back to life. The use of this language, the familiar phrases, could help give hope to the grieving persons.

By the time of writing this book, skyping, videoconferencing, FB, live streaming etc., were unheard of. While are necessary, they still cannot replace the vital role that physical presence plays in bringing about closure.

The possibility that the deceased is out of sight but is present somewhere else in the form of a spirit helps in the healing process. It is encouraging to know all is not lost. The idea that we can connect, even share a meal is not absurd within the Kikuyu group of peoples. They even used to pour some food and drink at the hearth to appease and seek communion with the spirits of the dead before they ate the food or took the drink.

This is popularly known as libation. Sacrifices were also offered to the spirits to keep them happy and to solicit for their blessings and protection in case of attacks by an enemy. It is difficult for someone who lives in a foreign land to feel connected with the family spirits when they are this far away. But having an understanding and supportive group can help one feel surrounded by people (spirits) that care.

It is from that understanding that we came up with a ritual that we thought would help us close our mourning. We had all brought to this session a photo of our deceased relative. Those who could get a copy of the eulogy that was read at the funeral service also brought it. Some brought copies of letters, emails and video clips that the deceased wrote or was featured in.

We put the photos on the table where we had put the bowl with sand and the cross. We all took some moments to look at the photos. We then took turns in reading each of the deceased's eulogy. Tears flowed! At times, the cries turned to shouts, but we all seemed to understand the situation. Some had prepared to read verses that their loved ones cherished, and some sang their favorite hymns and songs. Time seemed to have stood still. Those who had composed tributes to their loved ones read them out loud before their photograph. This tribute by Agnes (not her real name) stood out and is reproduced here by her permission:

My dear Mama
I will live to remember your love,
I will never forget how you brought me up.
You cared for me and supplied my needs,
you represented God to me.
Forgive me for not being there, to say
my final goodbye to you.
Forgive me for not being there,
when they lowered you into your final resting home.
If I had wings, I could fly,
but I am sure you will understand me mama.
Someday I'll see you,
someday soon I'll join you,
This time we will never separate again,
I love you, Mama.

We had simulated a funeral, and it felt like one to us. There was an aura of serenity around the whole thing. Our talking had turned to whispers and our motions were now calculated, even honorable, and very intentional. It looked so much like a real funeral. We were fully captivated by the sense of death. It seemed so real.

We then in silence put all the photos, eulogies, and tributes into a safe box, sealed it and put it in our archive. This was one of the most solemn moments I have ever experienced. It was watered with our tears, blessed by our love that we espoused to our loved ones during this moment of saying goodbye and burying our dead.

The assumption was that the exercise of acting out what we missed because we were not there to bury our loved ones was going to help us face the reality of their demise as well as avail us an opportunity for closure and subsequent healing. It is no wonder when the process was over and the group members were asked to name the highlight of the project, 7 out of the nine (I included) said this was the moment that had the heaviest impact on them. They all said it touched them to the core and acted as the most effective catalyst to their process of healing.

After the meal, we parted. It was around nine o'clock. No one had noticed the time pass. We were feeling like family who were there for each other. We were at home with each other. We hugged each other and then we left to meet again in another two weeks.

Session 4

We met again on January 7, 2010, at the usual hour of 4 o'clock. There was evidence of some enthusiasm about the group, some cohesion, some unity, some harmony that I cannot adequately explain in words. Wairuri led us in prayer and shared her reflection from Ps. 34:4-8. She reminded us that God hears our cries and comes to our rescue. God had seen our grief and had created this group/forum to rescue us from its anguish.

In this session, we were to respond to questions 16 and 17. We were also to try to work out a strategy of helping others both as individuals and as a community of faith. As individuals these suggestions were put forward. We can help others by:

- Forming support groups.
- Listening to them without criticizing them.

- Showing them that we care.
- Showing compassion to them.
- Being physically present and taking time to console them.
- Praying with those grieving and offering whatever other support that is necessary including financial support.
- Staying close to the bereaved for as long as it takes.
- Encouraging them to talk openly and honestly and to express their emotions and not cover them up.
- Encouraging them to eat well and to rest to keep themselves healthy.
- Helping create rituals and encouraging them to recall good times with the deceased.
- Encouraging them to be busy, to do exercises and other chores and to concentrate less on their pains.
- Encouraging them to seek help and to let others help them.
- Urging them to look to their faith community and to participate in its life because faith is a strong ally.

The group chose not to disband but to split into two groups of four, and with the pastor's assistance we formed two grief support groups. Each group was to invite others who have lost their loved ones. We also emphasized having rituals performed in the church. We also suggested that the pastor should conduct a memorial service for all the bereaved in which candles will be lit with each representing one of the deceased at the beginning of the service and extinguished at some point as each individual or family reads a goodbye tribute to their deceased person. I found that suggestion to be very powerful and promised to conduct a service annually beginning this year. The summary of the strategy is as follows:

a) To train the laity on how to do the activities suggested above. Use pastors and other professionals where necessary.
b) Form two grief support groups. These groups will meet weekly or bi-weekly for 4 to 8 sessions.
c) In the meantime, the group of 8 will continue meeting for fellowship and to do any unfinished business. They all volunteered to be trained. After training, the group will divide into two equal groups and then invite others to join.
d) The group will be present to help any bereaved persons whenever and wherever duty called.

Session 5

After strategizing, which was an arduous task, the group dismissed with prayer, looking forward to meeting for their last session. January 21, 2010, was our last day of meeting. This meeting was particularly geared towards measuring the success of the project. The first indicator of success and usefulness of the project was the enthusiasm shown by the participants.

None of them came to the meetings late and none missed any of the sessions. The group did not want to disband but requested to learn more and form grief support groups. The meeting opened with prayer and a short reflection on John 11:17-27, hinged on verse 25: "I am the resurrection and the life." These words were to point us to a re-union with our departed friends and relatives when Christ returns.

Each of the participants then shared their personal evaluations of the process:

- Was the process important for you? All said it was and as indicated above their full participation is a strong indicator.
- If it was valuable, why and how? The common response was that it helped them share their grief with others, a process that led to significant relief on their part. They found the fellowship, care, support, and presence vital to the process.
- How do you feel now? All had responded using the word, "Great!" Asked to elaborate what that means, our discussion seemed to mean, "I am better than when I first began."
- Has something changed from the time you started this process until now? "Yes" was the common response. Some said they felt stronger. Some said they felt less lonely. Some said they slept better and grieved less. Only one said that she felt she had now started to grief. Her denial (after 8 months) had come to an end, and she was now facing the reality of her brother's demise.
- How would you rate the process on a scale of 1-10 with 10 being the highest? Five rated it 10, three 9 and one 8. Asked to explain his rating of 8, he said he'd have wished the process to begin sooner, immediately after one loses her/his loved one(s). He thought our process was belated and came as an afterthought.

The measurement of success will fall on some key areas. The pastor will continue to observe how the participants will live out their lives in the future and how involved they will get in the plan of action outlined above. The development of a useful tool to use in the process might have to be put on hold. This will be developed gradually through the process of training.

In the meantime, a small brochure with a listing of some things one can do to assist those who are grieving is to be produced. The eight members have volunteered to train to be equipped with information and skills on how to manage grief support groups. This willingness and the high rating of the process no doubt speak volumes about the importance of the entire project.

The participants also let out their feelings in that safe space. They expressed their emotions freely and shamelessly displayed them. They freely and publicly expressed their weaknesses and inner concealed feelings. This meets one of the major goals of the book: to let go – talk it out- express it.

Personally, I became healed. The process gave me opportunity to grieve and share my feelings. I was able to finally bury my father. If I were to rate the success of the project, I would gave it 90% success if not more. The fact that a way has been opened to help more people who are or will become victims of mourning without the body makes this exercise such a worthwhile project.

I would not hesitate to recommend this process to pastors or spiritual caregivers who are shepherding or come across populations who grieve in isolation. Usually the majority of such people are immigrants, and I am sure the process will be helpful. You can modify the process to suit your circumstances. Anything that you may do to reach out and support those who suffer in silence and in isolation because they lacked an opportunity to bury their loved ones will be of great value.

Any encouraging word, time spent with them, praying for and with them, that action that shows you care, sharing stories with them will be highly invaluable. There are many out there who are groping for your support, a hand to hold them steady and a person to walk with them on their journey of pain and loss.

The Presence of the Divine

God was involved in the process. We felt God's presence as we shared the Word of God and more so in our healing. The hope that we now have cannot be given by anyone else. The pastor, himself a victim of the same predicament, experienced the graces of God in a spectacular way.

All that took place because of this group that came together in God's church. The church provided a safe and sacred space. The church provided the constituency with which to work with. Hopefully the formation of grief support groups will be a constant feature in the activities of our churches. The process has begun. The work has been documented. The process will no doubt continue.

Finally, we should come back to the bowl with the cross, sand, and small stones, each representing a member of the group. We were wondering what to do with it when one of the members had a great idea of preserving it. He suggested that we use cement on it to hold the sand and small stones together and to permanently hold the cross in place. This signified that we had been united under the cross.

We had worked together and together we had emerged stronger than when we first began. We have been built into a family of God under the cross of Jesus Christ, the healer of our pains, our wounds, our sorrows and our sufferings. On this firm foundation, others will build. This group of eight echoes the words of Jesus to Peter:

"And I tell you that you are Peter, and on this rock, I will build my church and the gates of Hades will not overcome it" (NIV. Matt 16:18, NIV).

This group has pioneered the grief support groups and I have no doubt their work will be felt and bring healing to many for years to come.

The church or faith community is the best place for the bereaved to run to. It is their city of refuge. The church is rich in three critical areas. It has the Word, the gospel. The church has the community. The church has trained personnel who can reach out and support the suffering. The church has the place for the rituals if necessary to bring healing.

With such riches, we can be of much help to immigrant communities that grope for support when death visits their own and cannot be there to say goodbye to them and with their kin during their funeral celebrations.

The problem I have tried to address is real and painful. My prayer and hope is that this book will provoke and move us to action. No one should grief and suffer in silence while living in a community of people of faith who have resources that they can employ to alleviate the suffering. That is at the heart of this book. Let us arise and grab that hand that is groping for support. Your support!

Conclusion

As noted elsewhere in the story of Mary, we have all dealt with grief in one way or another. Many books have been written about pain, hurt and grief. Grief is a part of life, and we are all prone to it. I am yet to meet someone who is immune to grief.

We are our brother's/sister's keeper. We need each other and this is something we cannot afford to neglect. When we stand with each other; see people around us; visit a grocery store and see the associates there who make our shopping possible; we feel taken care of. We need each other to make life possible and livable; to make it what it is. We mostly take it for granted that someone will be there for us, but when we consciously think about it, we realize how significant that is.

Pastors are shepherds. Pastors don't exist if there is no sheep. Pastors owe their name and job description, even their title from the existence of the sheep. The presence of the sheep defines our ministry. Yes, there are good shepherds and bad shepherds. This is how Jesus describes the good shepherd,

"But he who enters by the door is the shepherd of the sheep. To him the gatekeeper opens. The sheep hear his voice, and he calls his own sheep by name and leads them out. When he has brought out all his sheep, he goes before them and the sheep follow him, for they know his voice." (John 10: 2-5). He goes ahead and adds, "I am the good shepherd.

The good shepherd lays down his life for the sheep" (John 10: 11, ESV).

Pastors by their very nature and job, are shepherds. The question should be: How do they take care of their flock? We cannot afford to pick and choose the kind of care we need to give our flock (those under our charge). We are there to meet their needs, to motivate and rally others to provide help to those in need, to try as far as possible to address their concerns or griefs or even problems they may be facing. If we neglect this critical duty, or in other words, let some fall through the cracks, we would have abandoned if not failed in our work and ministry.

Ours is to care of the souls entrusted to us by God. Just as Jesus said in John 10: 18, (ESV), "... This charge I have received from my Father". We too have been given a charge, a divine charge from God the Father, "Feed, tend, take care of my sheep" (John 21:15, 16, 17, ESV). This is a charge that pastors need to take very seriously.

If a pastor neglects this crucial charge of caring for the flock, s/he is not fit to be in that office. S/he is not even worthy of that name. No title without responsibility has any tangible meaning. Pastors have a charge and must carry it out to the best of their ability without let or favor.

The church needs pastors critically in times of grief. Nothing causes greater grief than the loss of a loved one. This is an area that pastors need to give a lot of unreserved attention. That is when our members, their families, their friends and even their neighbors need us most. We have a duty to be there. We have no luxury to leave it to chance.

In the churches, the pastor, should be more sensitive to the "other". In our case, the other can be seen as not belonging. These terms are used carelessly to describe them: undocumented, illegal, foreigner, alien, and so on. These are not flattering titles especially if they are used particularly to describe an individual. The terms "kick one out of the group that belongs". They are alienating, and are actually used for that very purpose, to disenfranchise. Once internalized, they become demeaning and belittling. They make the individual so defined to feel like a lesser person. When all is well and you are not within this bracket, the sting felt by those within it might not have any effect on you. But if one is restricted in movement, and what they can do because they are the "other" the sting hurts like that of a scorpion.

Going back to the country where one originally came from, when it is extremely necessary to do so, is "the big one". The fact that you cannot without risking your return is a devastating thing even to think of it. That is not the only debilitating fear. I have listened to many testimonies of people who are in this category. They say even the very sight of a trooper makes them nervous.

Some have admitted they shake like a leaf in the wind if a trooper seems to be walking towards them. Some even panic and lose direction if a state trooper seems like s/he is following them or comes driving past them. It is disorienting and not a pleasant experience at all. Even if the trooper is on a very different mission, they are afraid of his presence.

They are afraid of anyone who looks like a policeman or associated with law enforcement. It becomes more horrifying if one is stopped by a policeman for a minor traffic offense. It becomes a traumatic experience, an experience that one is unlikely to forget. I have been there, so I know.

It is disarming to be called by a term that is derogatory. The phobia that comes with being "the other" deters one from even reporting crimes or molestation to law enforcers. Unfortunately, some of us use the condition of "being the other" to intimidate or take advantage of them. The thing they dread most is to go into a police station. In a nutshell, they dread anyone taking too much interest in them. Their lives are lived in an aura of fear and suspicion. They crave for the day that things will change and by God's miraculous intervention, they will be given papers.

When death strikes, and it does, and given the predicament they live in, it is more than obvious that they will dangle their arms seeking for support. This is where the community, the church and the pastor(s) come in. While the former two can provide generalized support, the pastor can give personal and professional help. The pastor's supporting hand speaks volumes.

Venturing out and being prominent without looking over one's shoulder are luxuries that the so called "other" do not enjoy. For some time now traveling is a big hassle for them especially if it involves going across states lines. The very idea of going through an airport or just close to a border is troubling. For some the last time they were at an airport was when they jetted into the country upon arrival from overseas.

For others, their routes are set, to work, to the store, to church, and back home. No more. They have and understandably so, no courage to be unnecessarily conspicuous unless there is no way to avoid it. It is as if it is anathema to expose oneself to any situation that can endanger their existence.

How do we support such people who find themselves in such double tragedy? This tool can be useful. The tool is based on the experience of a particular group of people from central Kenya, the Gikuyu. However, their experiences can cut across the board.

Most other immigrants are generally in the same situation. The tool can act as a guide. The caregivers can modify it to suit their particular environments. The specific principle is that the sufferers/victims need help. We need to help and support them. That is the sole and one objective of this book.

Help that dangling hand looking for support. This book gives you some direction. At least you can be in a position of starting from somewhere. My hope and prayer are that we will be supportive of those who are seeking for your/my support. Look out for that arm and when you see it, please help. The owner is groping for support.

The End

Bibliography

Bartel, Mark. What is Spiritual? What is Spiritual Suffering? "The Journal of Pastoral Care and Counseling." Vol. 58, No. 3, Fall 2004

Bonhoeffer, Dietrich. Life Together: The Classic Exploration of Faith in Community. New York: Harper Collins Publishers, 1954. Claypool, John. Mending the Heart. Chicago, IL: Cowley Publications, 1999.

Clinebell, Howard. Basic Types of Pastoral Care and Counseling: Resources for the Ministry of Healing and Growth. Nashville: Abingdon Press, 1984.

Corey, Gerald. Theory and Practice of Counseling and Psychotherapy, Sixth Edition. Belmont, CA: Wadsworth, 2001.

Culbertson, Phillip. Counseling and Christian Wholeness: Caring for God's People. Minneapolis: Fortress Press, 2000.

Davis, Randy. Letting Go with Love. Los Angeles: St Martin's Press, 1987. Detrich, L. Richard. How to Recover from Grief. Valley forge, PA: Judson Press, 1996

Dittes, James E. Pastoral Counseling: The Basics. Louisville, KY: Westminster John Knox Press, 1999.

Donovan, Daniel. A Time of Grace: One Family's Experience with Chronic Care. New York: Paulist Press, 1990.

Egan, Gerard. The Skilled Helper: A Problem-Management and Opportunity-Development Approach to Helping, Seventh Edition. Pacific Grove, CA: Wadsworth Group Publishers, 2002.

First Presbyterian Church of Atlanta. FPC Care Ministry. Graham, Larry Kent. Care of Persons, Care of Worlds: A Psychosystems Approach to Pastoral Care and Counseling. Nashville: Abingdon Press, 1992.

Jensen, Amy Hillyard. Healing Grief, Third edition. Redmond, WA: Medic Publishing Co., 1999.

Kalas, J. Ellsworth. If Experience is Such a Good Teacher Why Do I Keep Repeating the Course? Nashville, TN: Dimensions for Living, 2001.

Kenyatta, Jomo. Facing Mount Kenya, Second Edition. Nairobi, Kenya: 1938.

Kubler-Ross, Elisabeth. Death, The Final Stage of Growth. Englewood Cliffs, NJ: Prentice Hall, 1975.

--------- On Death and Dying. New York: Mac Millan, 1969.

Lierop, van Peter. Pastoral Counseling: A Comprehensive Text for Pastors, Counselors,Teachers. Nairobi, Kenya: The Christian teachers Educational Association, 1992.

Lewis, C.S. A Grief Observed. NY: Seabury Press, 1961. Malcolm, Jack. "Little Churches Have a Lot to Offer."Presbyterians Today, December 2003.

Mbiti, John S. African Religions and Philosophy. Nairobi, Kenya: Heinemann, 1969.

McGoldrick, Monica and Betty Carter, eds. The Expanded Family Life Cycle, Individual, Family and Social Perspectives. Needham Heights, MA: Allyn and Bacon, 1999.

Menden Hall, Laura. "On Earth as It Is in Heaven: Reconciliation Through and with Justice," in PCUSA. General Assembly Report, 2001.

Moore, James W. If You're Going the Wrong Way...Turn Around! How to Head in God's Direction. Nashville, TN: Dimensions for Living, 2004.

------- Is There Life After Stress? Nashville, TN: Dimension for Living, 1992.

Mugambi, J.N.K. African Christian Theology: An Introduction.

Nairobi, Kenya: Heinemann, 1989. African Heritage and Contemporary Christianity. Nairobi, Kenya: Heinemann, 1989. Ed. Christian Mission and Social Reformation. Nairobi, Kenya: Heinemann, 1989 The Biblical Basis for Civilization: Theological Reflections Based on an African Experience. Nairobi, Kenya: Heinemann, 1989.

Muita, Isaiah Wahome. Hewn from Quarry: The Presbyterian Church of East Africa 100 Years and Beyond. Nairobi, Kenya: 2003.

Myss, Caroline. Why People Don't Heal and How They Can. New York: Harmony Books, 1997.

National Institutes of Mental Health. Anxiety Disorders. NIH Publication, Sept.2002.

O'Connor, Nancy. Letting Go with Love: The Grieving Process. Apache Junction, AR: La Mariposa Press, 1984.

Paget, Naomi K and Janet R. McCormack. The Work of the Chaplain. Valley Forge, PA: Judson Press, 2006.

Poe, Harry Lee. Christian Witness in a Postmodern World. Nashville: Abingdon Press, 2001.

Popcak, Gregory K. God Help Me! These People are driving Me Nuts: Making Peace With Difficult People. Chicago: Loyola Press, 2001.

Price, Wayne W. In Transition: Navigating Life's Major Changes. Harrisburg, PA: Morehouse Publishing, 2002.

Ramsay, Nancy J. Pastoral Diagnosis: A Resource for Ministries of Care and Counseling. Minneapolis: Fortress Press, 1998.

Rando, Therese A. How to Go on Living when Someone You Love Dies. Lexington, MA: Lexington Books, 1991.

Roberts,Rabbi Stephen. Professional Spiritual & Pastoral Care: A Practical Clergy and Chaplain's Handbook. Woodstock, VT: Skylight Paths, 2013.

Schuller, Robert H. Tough Times Never Last, But Tough People Do! New York: Bantam Books, 1984.

Simonton, Carl O. Getting Well Again. New York: Bantam Books, 1992.

Steinke, Peter L. How Your Church Family Works: Understanding Congregations as Emotional Systems. Herndon, VA: The Alban Institute, 2006.

Taylor, Charles W. The Skilled Pastor: Counseling as the Practice of Theology. Minneapolis: Fort Press, 2001.

Walker, Theodore, Jr. Empower the People: Social Ethics for the African American - Church. Maryknoll, NY: Orbis Books, 1991.

Westberg, Granger. Good Grief. Minneapolis, MN: Fortress Press, 1997.

Whelan, Gloria. A Time to Keep Silent. Grand Rapids, MI: William B. Eerdmans, 1993.

Wimberly, Edward P. Recalling Our Own Stories: Spiritual Renewal for Religious Caregivers. San Francisco, CA: Jossey-Bass Publishers, 1997.

Worden, J. William. Grief Counseling and Grief Therapy (Third Edition). A Handbook for the Mental Health Practitioner. New York, NY: Springer Publishing Company, 2002.

Yancey, Philip. Where is God When it Hurts? Grand Rapids, MI: Zondervan Press, 1990

Internet Sources

About.Com. Understanding the Grieving Process- Seven Phases of the Grieving

Process.http://lungdiseases.about.com/od/endoflifeissuescare/a/7grief steps.htm?p=1

Center for Grief and Healing. Myths and Facts about Grief.www. griefandhealing.org.

Center got Grief and Healing. Taking care of Yourself. www. griefandhealing.org.

Center for Grief and Healing. The Stages of Grief. http://www. griefandhealing.org.

Cyber Recovery Fellowship Forums. Starting Over After Loss-Overcoming Grief.

http://www.cyberrecovery.net/forums/showthread.php?t=2288.

Good News Magazine. "Steps in Dealing with Grief," in What Happens After Death. http://www.gnmagazine.org/booklets/ad/grief.htm.

Medical News Today. www.medicalnewstoday.com.

Memorial Hospital. The Stages of Grief. Towanda, PA. http://www. memorialhospital. org/library/general/stress/THE-3.html.Ossefort-Russell, Candyce. Grief Questionnaire. http://www.candycecounseling. com/questionnaire.html.

PCUSA World Mission. Highlights. Winter/Spring 2009. Shera, Katherine and Susan

Essock. Brief Grief Questionnaire. Boston. http://www.bostongrief. com/id6.html.

The Gilroy Dispatch. Three Steps to Overcoming Grief and Loss. http://www. gilroydispatch.com/printer/article.asp?c=196669.

Tsunami Survivors Experienced Complex and Grieving Process. Coping with Death and Dying. Understanding the Grieving Process: Coping with Death- Phases of Grief.

http://www.medicalnewstoday.com/printerfriendlynews.php? newsid=121020.

United Church of God, an Int. Assoc. Steps in Dealing With Grief. http://www.ucgstp.

org/lit/booklets/death/death06.htm.

University at Buffalo. Counseling Services. http://ub-counseling. buffalo.edu/process. shtml.

University of Iowa, University Counseling Services. Coping with Death, Grief, and Loss. http://www.uiowa.edu-ucs/griefloss.html.

What can you do to Help Someone Who is Grieving. http://www. griefandhealing.org.

Appendices

Appendix 1

QUESTIONAIRE: Mourning without the Body.

Recently you had a sad experience after losing your loved one(s). I am writing this book that hopefully in the near future will be helpful to those who will perhaps experience a similar loss like you had. This experience is particularly important to those who are not able to physically be present to witness the last funeral and burial rites of their loved ones. Your experience will go a long way in helping others whose experience is not dissimilar to your own.

Please answer as clearly, briefly, and honestly as you can. Return the filled questionnaire in the stamped return envelope provided with the address label on it.

[NB. Your name will not be used in the dissertation without your express permission.] If you need more space, feel free to attach extra sheets to the questionnaire.

1. How did you receive the news?
2. Had you any warnings something "bad" was going to happen prior to the death(s)?
3. Describe briefly what the warnings were if your answer to question 2 is yes.
4. What was your first reaction?
5. With whom did you share the news?

6. Who mourned with you?
7. Was the community/family/church support helpful to you?
8. How did it help you?
9. Was there anything negative about this support?
10. How did you feel about not viewing or being present with the family for the funeral and burial?
11. Have you overcome your grief?
12. If yes, how long did it take to overcome it?
13. If not, how strong is it?
14. What did you find most helpful in overcoming the grief?
15. What did you find least helpful?
16. What can you say to someone in similar circumstances?
17. How can the church/community help in supporting those in grief?

members responded to the pastor's call while others who read of the sad story on www.AjabuAfrica.com shared the information

Appendix 2

Questionnaire for Pastors

Hello brother in the Lord:

I am in the process of writing a book. The book addresses the issue of bereavement for those in the diaspora who have left part of their families in the country where they came from. Some of those, for a variety of reasons, are not able to travel back to where they came from when someone dies. They are therefore not able to moan with the others, grieve with the family or participate physically in the funeral and burial process. They grieve in isolation. Sometimes they never close.

You have been a pastor with such families or individuals. Attached is a questionnaire. Please fill it out for me. Your contribution will be acknowledged in the manual when it is published. Please focus on the people from your country of origin who have lost their loved ones and were not able to travel. Be as comprehensive as you possibly can.

Thanking you and God bless you and your ministry in a mighty way.

Rev. Dr. Joseph Kimatu

When a Loved One Passes on Overseas and You are not able to Travel

a) What is the initial response of the bereaved? What emotions are apparent?
b) As a pastor what is your initial response/intervention and what do you initiate?
c) How does the church respond?
d) How does the community respond?
e) Are there any set procedures in your church for long term care to families whose loved ones pass overseas?
f) Are there any special rituals that the bereaved or the church do console the family or the bereaved?
g) For families who are not able to travel for funeral and burial of their loved one(s), is there any special care that you provide to them?
h) How does not being able to travel affect the bereaved as opposed to those who are able to travel?
i) Does your church have a "Grief/Bereavement Support Group"? How helpful is it to those unable to travel?
j) What workable advice would you give to the church in order for it to be helpful to those grieving and unable to travel to join their families for funeral/burial observances?
k) What else do you think is helpful to such a group?
l) What reasons cause the inability of those unable to travel?

N.B. (Please be as comprehensive as you possibly can. Feel free to add whatever you think is important for this research. Where possible give particular cases, without the names of course).

Please mail the questionnaire to Rev. Dr. Joseph Kimatu, 331 Naismith St., Springfield, MA 01104 or scan/send as word doc using the email…kimatu07a@hotmail.com

Appendix 3

When A Loved One Passes Overseas and You are not able to Travel

1. What is the initial response of the bereaved? What emotions are apparent?

   The initial response is a deep feeling of a big lost. Being away when good celebrations are happening back in their countries is something that the immigrant can handle more easily. But is so difficult to handle with the feelings of the loss of a beloved one. They wanted to be close to their relatives for mutual support. Being away increases the feeling of lost.

   Also, thinking about those who has been away from their countries for many years, they also have the feeling of guiltiness for not be able to give emotional support for their relatives on time of sufferings. They feel guilty for not being able to give the last hug or last kiss to the people who passed away.

2. As a pastor what is your initial response/intervention and what do you initiate?

   Depending of who I'm going to give support. People react differently on this kind of situation. But, in general, I allow then to put away their feelings and, as they are doing that, I try to let them to bring to their mind the good memories that will be forever in their hearts as it was at the heart of the deceased person.

3. How does the church respond?

   I was pastor of a church of immigrants here in the USA for 10 years. The church response was firstly through the companionship, practicing what the bible teaches us to do, weeping with those who weep. In some cases, it's possible that the church helps their family back in their country providing some financial support for funeral. This can happen also when the deceased person lived here. But I believe that the companionship is the best way to give support to the bereaved.

4. How does the community respond?

   When the community is called to support it has done in a very good way. The solidarity is strong in times of this kind of suffering. When it is needed, the church may do some kind of activity, like a special kind of fundraising food. The support is not only from the church's members, but from the outsiders too.

5. Are there any set procedures in your church for long term care to families whose loved ones pass overseas?

   I never have something like that.

6. Are there any special rituals that the bereaved or the church do console the family or the bereaved?

   We used to do a special service in memoriam, that could be at the church facility or at the bereaved's home.

7. For families who are not able to travel for funeral and burial of their loved one(s), is there any special care that you provide to them?

   This kind kind of situation is very common. Usually, the family could not to travel because their immigration status. Beside the funeral service, as the pastor, I used to visit several times the bereaved family or person, but not only me, other members of the church also would do the same. This is important in order to let those in lost not feel loneliness.

8. How does not being able to travel affect the bereaved as opposed to those who are able to travel?

I believe that the feeling of grief will last longer, because they were not able to do the ritual to give back to the "dust what was dust".

9. Does your church have a "Grief/Bereavement Support Group"? How helpful is it to those unable to travel?

No, I didn't have a special group. I believe that in situation like that a group were formed spontaneously.

10. What workable advice would you give to the church in order for it to be helpful to those grieving and unable to travel to join their families for funeral/ burial observances?

A special service in memoriam would be very helpful. Also, as in many cases their families back in their respective countries are pour, provide some financial support to be sent to their families would give to those who are here and unable to travel the feeling that they are doing something, and they are being useful.

11. What else do you think is helpful to such a group?

12. What reasons cause the inability of those unable to travel?

Financial problems, time's inability and immigration status. For time's inability I mean that in some countries, the law order that the deceased shall be buried in hours. So, there is no ample time to arrive before the funeral.

Printed in the United States
by Baker & Taylor Publisher Services